Tiger

Tiger

The Life of Tipu Sultan

Kate Brittlebank

juggernaut

JUGGERNAUT BOOKS
KS House, 118 Shahpur Jat, New Delhi 110049, India

First published by Juggernaut Books 2016

ISBN 9788193237298

Typeset in Adobe Caslon Pro by R. Ajith Kumar, New Delhi

Printed at Manipal Technologies Ltd

To the memory of my godfather
Roy C. Gregson

A man of infectious curiosity

Contents

Timeline

c. 1720	Haidar Ali born
1750	Tipu Sultan born, 20 November
1751–52	Siege of Tiruchirappalli
1761	Haidar secures total power in Mysore
1767	Outbreak of First Anglo-Mysore War
	Tipu receives first military command
1769	First Anglo-Mysore War ends
1774	Tipu marries first two wives
1780	Outbreak of Second Anglo-Mysore War
	Battle of Pollilur

1782	Death of Haidar: Tipu assumes power
1784	End of Second Anglo-Mysore War
1785	Kodagu rebellion crushed
1786	Embassy to Ottoman Sultan sails from Malabar coast
	Earl Cornwallis appointed British governor-general of India
	Marathas invade northern Mysore
1787	Tipu concludes peace with Marathas
	Embassy to French king departs
1788	Kodagu rebels: regains most of its territory
1789	Embassy to French king arrives home
1790	Embassy to Ottoman Sultan arrives home
	Outbreak of Third Anglo-Mysore War
1792	End of Third Anglo-Mysore War: princes taken hostage

1794	Princes return to Mysore
1797	Lord Mornington appointed British governor-general of India
1798	Tipu's embassy reaches Mauritius; French governor issues proclamation
	Proclamation published in Calcutta newspaper
1799	British and allies invade Mysore: Tipu killed 4 May

1

Myth vs Reality

Windsor Castle, a popular tourist destination not far from London, is an ancient seat of the British royal family. On days when the grand galleries, with their splendid royal portraits and luxurious furnishings, are open to the public, the visitor can view a number of cabinets displaying items from the Queen's collection, many acquired as gifts from loyal subjects to whichever sovereign sat upon the throne. Naturally, for a monarch, only the most magnificent of objects would do. Around two hundred years ago, a number of Indian artefacts came into the collection, presented to George III and his successors. They were war loot, seized after the fall of Srirangapattana, the capital of Mysore, in 1799; all had belonged to Tipu Sultan, the late ruler of that kingdom.

The most stunning of the objects in the cabinets is the life-sized gold tiger's head that formed part of Tipu's throne, known colloquially as the 'Massy Tiger'. Crystal teeth bared, it glares through the glass as if permanently outraged by its owner's inglorious end. Nearby is one of Tipu's war banners; made of green velvet, it is decorated with a stylised calligraphic tiger mask. Deciphered, the calligraphy reads *asad allah ul-ghalib*, 'the victorious lion of God'. Among other items of loot gifted to the British king were a jewel-encrusted *huma* bird that had stood atop the canopy of the throne, a war dress and helmet, a cotton tent panel patterned with tiger stripes, some velvet palanquin cushions, again with tiger stripes and embroidered in silk and gold, and one of Tipu's seals. But this was only a tiny fraction of the vast amount of plunder seized by the victorious troops in the aftermath of Tipu's death. So extensive was the looting, numerous artefacts associated with him can be found scattered across the British Isles in museums and other collections. From the National Museum of Scotland in Edinburgh to Powis Castle in Wales to the Victoria and Albert Museum in London, today's tourist can see displays of Tipu memorabilia from the martial to the mundane.

For thirty years, first Haidar Ali, Tipu's father, then Tipu himself, had been at the forefront of the British public's consciousness. Terrifying tales of attacks on British forces and threats to trading settlements such as Madras appeared in the newspapers of the day, embellished by distance as they were carried home by sea. Over the decades and through four Anglo-Mysore wars, people hungrily awaited reports of the latest outrage perpetrated by the so-called tyrants. The return of British prisoners of war, some of whom had been held captive in Mysore for several years, led to the writing of books that told harrowing stories of hardship and torture. That many of these accounts were self-serving was of little interest to their avid readers. So by the time he died at the hands of General Harris's troops, as they besieged his island capital in 1799, Tipu Sultan was possibly the most famous Indian, if not villain, in the United Kingdom.

Not surprisingly, celebrations in Britain at the news of Tipu's demise fuelled further creative output on the part of not only authors and playwrights but also artists, who put paint to canvas to glorify the victory. Careers were launched and some ended. Arthur Wellesley, later to become the Duke of Wellington, famous for defeating Napoleon at the Battle of Waterloo, was placed in charge of Srirangapattana and then went on to overcome the Marathas in 1803, at the Battle of Assaye. India was Wellesley's proving ground. The governor-general, Lord Mornington, who was Arthur's older brother Richard, did not fare so well. Having ordered the attack on Mysore in defiance of his political masters at home, and despite energetic attempts by his supporters to vindicate him, his only reward was an undistinguished Irish peerage and retirement. Well into the nineteenth century, the infamous figure of Tipu Sultan held sway in the public mind. As late as 1868, Wilkie Collins chose the siege of Srirangapattana and its subsequent looting as the setting for the opening of his bestselling novel *The Moonstone*.

One has to wonder what Tipu would have made of it all. Also, would he have cared? Very probably, he would. To terrorise his enemies was his goal and in that he had succeeded, not only through his actions but also by his clever use of imagery and symbolism. Although he did not realise it, his choice of the tiger motif for his insignia resonated strongly with the British, whose own emblem is the lion. It is no coincidence that the Seringapatam medal, awarded to those who had taken part in the siege, depicts a rampaging lion mauling a supine tiger. The ecstatic celebrations would also have confirmed in Tipu's mind that he had been correct in his assumption that the East India Company's expansionist activities were a credible threat to the freedom of the subcontinent's inhabitants, that he was the last bulwark against British imperial desires. It is this prescience that distinguishes Tipu and his father from their contemporaries. With Tipu gone, the Company was able, in his own words, to 'fix [its] talons' ever deeper into Indian soil.

Local rulers and chiefs, such as the Nizam of Hyderabad or the Maratha Peshwa, frequently failed to recognise the danger posed by allowing British Residents – ostensibly ambassadors but in truth much more than that – to be assigned to their courts. In contrast, Europeans were forbidden from entering Mysore territory uninvited, for whatever purpose, on threat of imprisonment. Those who did make the mistake of crossing the boundaries of the realm soon found themselves in difficulties, sometimes forced into military employment even if they were completely untrained. When one man who ended up in this position – an English clerk who had unwittingly wandered across Mysore's border – protested that he had no skill in warfare, Haidar responded that he 'never doubted the soldiership of a man who wore a Hatt', and proceeded to recruit him. The Mysore ruler and his son understood all too well that what set European armies apart from Indian troops was their technical expertise and superior discipline, and they set about correcting the imbalance through the use of French mercenaries.

Haidar and Tipu's closely guarded borders meant that their adversaries were forced to rely on second-hand reports, usually from spies. One of the tasks of the Company's Residents at Indian courts, such as Hyderabad or Pune, was the recruitment and management of secret agents. They also monitored reports the Indian rulers received from their own informants. As is always the case with espionage, the risk of betrayal and double-cross was ever-present, as well as unfounded rumour. In such an environment, of subterfuge and incomplete information, threats can be magnified, feeding the existing paranoia about the enemy's intentions. By the time Lord Mornington made the decision to order the invasion of Mysore in February 1799, any semblance of reality concerning the threat Tipu posed had long been lost from sight.

But since this book is about Tipu Sultan's life rather than his death, should we be concerned with how he was perceived by his enemy? At one level, such perceptions are little more than what might nowadays be referred to as 'colour and movement' – they tell us virtually nothing about who Tipu really was. At another level, though, it is useful to be aware of the mythmaking surrounding this controversial figure, so as to avoid the pitfalls associated with believing the propaganda. We cannot understand the past by viewing it through the prism of the present; hindsight is proverbially described as 'a wonderful thing' but it can also be a hindrance.

~

Let us imagine, then, what it might have been like to have been alive in south India in the second half of the eighteenth century. It is many decades since the great empire of the Mughals, who had dominated the political and financial affairs of the subcontinent for over 150 years, slipped into decline. New powers have risen and fallen, carved out of the remnants of the old empire: Arcot in the south, for example, Bengal and Awadh in the north. But you only know this if you are a member of the literate elite. If you are a peasant, such matters are irrelevant – instead your interests are related to survival and being left in peace. The life of the peasant revolves around the seasons, planting and harvests, and the small daily religious rituals that bring comfort to what is an often arduous existence. Most of all, you do not want the land you till laid waste by war. For this you look to whoever is in power and has control over all aspects of your life. You are not so concerned if he calls himself a Sunni or a Shi'a, a Vaishnava or a Shaivite; more important is that he (rarely but occasionally a 'she') does not impose unreasonable taxes and provides protection from attack. This last is particularly crucial if you have the misfortune to live in, or close to, disputed territory.

If you are a town-dweller, a merchant, say, your interests are different, especially if business is suffering as a result of the entry into your markets of a new competitor, one that is making inroads into the spice and textile trades: the Europeans, who you will know as 'hat-wearers' and who have established footholds at a number of points along the coast. The hat-wearers are showing worrying signs of aggression and are ignorant of the correct ways of men. Although you try to avoid having to deal with them, there are some in your community who believe there may be advantages in doing so. As time goes on, you realise that the hat-wearers are not all the same; they have different loyalties and speak a range of languages. Conflict breaks out between them, involving local rulers who take opposing sides. It is hard to know how to respond to these developments.

And if you are of a military inclination, an

ambitious adventurer perhaps, a man like Haidar Ali, you have used your considerable abilities to work your way into power, first as a soldier in the forces of Mysore, then as *faujdar* of the fort of Dindigul (in present-day Tamil Nadu) – at that time part of the Wodeyars' Mysore kingdom – and on up the ladder of rewards, until you have removed all opposition and seized control of the realm. But you do not proclaim yourself ruler. Throughout your initially tenuous but later firm control of the kingdom, you rule in the name of Krishna Raja Wodeyar II and his successors, the latter selected by you as children and virtually your prisoners. To the outside world, you maintain the fiction that you are merely the Dalavai or commander-in-chief of Mysore. But all who see and understand the true situation know that you are in charge, referring to you variously as 'Haidar Naik' or 'Nawab'. For all intents and purposes you are the king and are recognised as such – you wield the *danda*, the rod of force, a defining attribute of kingship. In 1763, you seize the wealthy city of Bednur, formerly the seat of the Ikkeris, who had ruled the area, in modern western Karnataka, for several centuries. You rename it Haidarnagar and issue coins in your name. You set about establishing a dynasty.

~

If we are to achieve an understanding of Tipu Sultan, therefore, we must first acknowledge that the world into which he was born was very different from our own. The British Raj had not come into being and the social upheaval resulting from the Industrial Revolution, becoming evident in Britain – mass migrations from villages to cities, the decline of cottage industries and specialised skills, the poverty and hardship of factory work – had yet to reach the subcontinent. The land itself was still comprised of regional powers, some more vibrant than others. The encroachment of the Europeans had been going on for over two centuries but only in the past few decades had

British influence begun to press inland, initially along the Ganges from Bengal into Awadh. The East India Company and its acolytes increasingly meddled in local succession disputes, as did the French, working their way into the political fabric of the region – in south India on the Coromandel and Malabar coasts, and later in the Deccan. Unlike these weakly defended areas, Mysore under Haidar Ali was in a strong position. The Eastern and Western Ghats provided a formidable barrier to would-be invaders of the kingdom. From the late 1750s, when Haidar came to power, and on into the 1780s, there was no reason for the population of Mysore, or its chiefs, to believe that the pattern of life – as it had done for centuries – would not continue along its familiar path. None could have foreseen the dramatic changes wrought by European imperial ambition and the impact of colonialism.

It is against this backdrop, then, that the following chapters examine Tipu's life, placing him, as someone who lived during the period just described, within his Indian and historical contexts. The book is not concerned with the consequences of his death, nor with what Europeans thought of him. Instead, it considers how Tipu perceived himself and why he acted in certain ways at certain times. It will, if you like, immerse the reader in his world, that of eighteenth-century south India. In doing so, the book recognises that a range of factors, both internal and external, influenced Tipu's choices and decisions as ruler of Mysore. It shows how he drew upon recognised kingly symbols and behaviour to reinforce his legitimacy to rule; it looks at how he dealt with the changes in fortune that British military successes against him brought about. And, lastly – given that he was not only a king but also a son, a husband and a father – it asks who was Tipu the man?

2

Son of the Soil

Many readers will know that Tipu Sultan is a controversial figure in India today. Much of the controversy stems from the fact that Tipu was the Muslim ruler of a kingdom whose subjects were predominantly non-Muslim: Hindus of varying persuasions, as well as the community of Jains centred on Shravanabelgola. Linked to that characterisation is the notion that he and his father were thus foreigners in the south. Yet it was the conquering British, not the Wodeyar dynasty of Mysore deposed by Haidar Ali, who had focused on the religious differences between ruler and ruled. In contrast, the Hindu Wodeyars' grievance was that they had lost power and they wanted it returned – that those who had seized it from them were adherents of the Muslim faith was secondary. They had ruled Mysore from the end of the fourteenth century, first as petty chiefs under the suzerainty of Vijayanagara, then independently from 1565 when that empire began to break up.

The hostile rhetoric of the British drew upon imagery with deep roots in Europe. As a result of the old animosity between Christendom and Islam, which had begun with the Crusades, the emphasis on Haidar and Tipu as 'Mahomedans' would have resonated strongly with their non-Indian audience. However, the Mughal domination of virtually the entire subcontinent and the empire's subsequent disintegration into successor states, as well as the presence of earlier Muslim dynasties in the Deccan, such as the Bahmanis of Gulbarga and Bidar, the Adil Shahis of Bijapur and the Qutb Shahis of Golconda, meant that the Indian peninsula had seen no small number of Muslims governing non-Muslim subjects. Haidar and Tipu's rule, therefore, was not a historical aberration – it was typical of the regional powers that arose during the eighteenth century. Furthermore, both Tipu and his father can be described as 'sons of the soil'; Tipu Sultan was the third generation of his family to be born south of the Vindhyas.

Contemporary accounts give the date of Tipu Sultan's birth as 20 Zil-Hijja 1163 AH, that is 20 November 1750 CE. Through the paternal line, Tipu's ancestry was predominantly Arab, specifically Navayat. Elite Muslims of Arab descent, the Navayats had been in south India for several centuries by the time Haidar Ali was born around 1720 to a Navayat mother. Haidar's father Fath Muhammad was the son of Muhammad Ali, who had migrated to Bijapur from north India with his father, Sheikh Wali Muhammad, during the reign of the Bijapur sultan Muhammad Adil Shah (r.1626–56). Once in the Deccan, Sheikh Wali formed a connection with the Gulbarga shrine of Bandanawaz Gesudaraz and arranged for Muhammad Ali to marry a daughter of one of the shrine's servants. The couple had four sons, including Fath Muhammad, Tipu's grandfather. Although we know nothing of Sheikh Wali's antecedents, he is reported to have come to India by sea; this, and the fact that his descendants intermarried with Navayats, suggests his family too were of Arab origin.

When conflict broke out between Bijapur and the Mughals at the start of the reign of Ali Adil Shah (r.1657–72), Muhammad Ali moved his family to Kolar in Sira, north-east of Bangalore, to escape the turmoil. His descendants remained in the south, in military service, moving periodically between Kolar, Arcot and Mysore. Fath Muhammad, like his father before him, was a soldier; and while in the employ of the Nawab of Sira, in command of the fort of Dodballapur, his second son, Haidar Ali, was born. Following Fath Muhammad's death a few years later, his widow sought refuge with her late husband's nephew in Mysore, and she and her two young sons settled in the capital, on the Kaveri river island of Srirangapattana.

As was the custom, the contemporary sources emphasise Tipu's paternal lineage, so not a great deal is known about his maternal line. He was born at Devanhalli, north of Bangalore (now the site of Bengaluru International Airport), a year or so after Mysore had captured the town from the Marathas, an action in which Haidar had distinguished himself and been rewarded with the title Khan. Tipu's mother, Fatima, also known as Fakhr un-Nissa, was the daughter of the governor of the fort of Cuddapah, in present-day Andhra Pradesh; she was Haidar's second wife. The Nawabs of Kurnool and Cuddapah were Pathans, which suggests that this branch of Tipu's family was too.

Although Sheikh Wali's male descendants turned to soldiering to earn their living, through marriage they retained their links with Sufism. Haidar's Navayat mother was the daughter of a *pirzada* from Thanjavur and his first wife the daughter of a *pirzada* from Sira. When Fakhr un-Nissa had learnt of her second pregnancy, she and Haidar had visited the shrine of Tipu Mastan Auliya in Arcot, to pray for a successful birth. They named their son Tipu Sultan Fath Ali Khan, Tipu after the saint and Fath Ali in recognition of his grandfather.

~

Shortly after Tipu was born, Haidar Ali began his rise through the ranks of the Mysore army of the Wodeyars. It was his achievements against the Marathas at Devanhalli that led to his deployment at the siege of Tiruchirappalli in 1751–52, when Mysore allied itself with British forces during the succession dispute for the Nawabship of the Carnatic, whose capital was Arcot in northern Tamil Nadu. Subsequently, Mysore switched sides to the French, as a result of British broken promises. Although Mysore did not achieve the territorial gains that it had hoped for, Haidar's involvement in this conflict allowed him for the first time to observe at close quarters European troops in action. It also led to his appointment as *faujdar* of the fort of Dindigul, where he subdued rebellious local chieftains known as *poligars* and brought peace to the region. It was also at Dindigul that he began employing French artillerymen and organising his troops along European lines, bringing order and discipline to the soldiers he commanded.

By the time Tipu was nine years old, Haidar had made his first move to seize power in Mysore. In 1759 he came to the support of Krishna Raja Wodeyar II, who was under the thumb of his commander-in-chief Nanjaraja Kalale. Only four years earlier, the Kalale family had conspired unsuccessfully to overthrow the Raja, indicating the precarious nature of the Wodeyars' position at this time. Haidar's intervention in the dispute between the ruling dynasty and the powerful Kalale family left the Raja beholden to him and virtually his puppet.

Within a year, though, Haidar faced a challenge

from the Dowager Rani, Lakshmi Ammani, a widow of Krishna Raja Wodeyar I, who conspired with the Mysore Diwan, Khande Rao, to dislodge him. In August 1760, just before Tipu turned ten, Haidar fled Srirangapattana for Bangalore, leaving behind his family captive within the fort. But almost a year later, having regrouped, he had retaken the island capital and a subdued Krishna Raja II admitted final defeat, requesting only that he be left with enough land to provide a pension. The Dowager Rani, however, did not give in so easily and continued her campaign to oust first Haidar, then Tipu, intriguing with external allies, including the British, right up until Tipu's death.

It is tempting to wonder how these developments might have affected Tipu: being held prisoner at such a young age, witnessing the rise and decline in his father's fortunes, observing the treachery of Khande Rao. One can imagine that as an intelligent boy he learnt from the experience, resolving perhaps never to forget how quickly fortune can change. He was certainly of an age to understand what was unfolding around him; from then on, until he could himself be a participant, he undoubtedly watched carefully as his father took steps to secure his position. Less than two years later Haidar captured Bednur. The city's wealth was derived from its position at the convergence of the trade routes from Malabar to the Western Ghats, and its possession provided the means for Haidar to stamp his own mark upon the Mysore realm. Practically, he did this by making the organisational changes referred to earlier: minting coins in his own name and renaming Bednur as Haidarnagar, as well as introducing new weights and measures within the town. He also looked to the education of his son. If Tipu were to inherit, he should not just take on his father's mantle but also build on his legacy – for that, he should be educated as a prince. It is likely therefore that, as well as the usual subjects of Qur'an, Islamic jurisprudence and hadiths, languages, philosophy and science, an emphasis would have been placed on Tipu studying history and what are known as 'mirrors for princes', treatises on government and kingship.

~

Scholarship, though, was only one aspect of the education of a future king; it was essential also that he be instructed in the art of warfare. For this task, Haidar appointed a loyal officer, Ghazi Khan, as his son's military preceptor, to accompany, guide and watch over him whenever the young man was in the field. Tipu's first experience of battle occurred when at the age of fifteen he took part in an action against a recalcitrant local chief, the *poligar* of Balam, whose territory lay not far from Bednur. As a result of his reported bravery and initiative, Tipu received his first honours from his father, the command of 500 horses and an assignment of lands in Mysore and Tamil Nadu, including Malvalli and Konanur. But it was the outbreak of the First Anglo-Mysore War in 1767 that provided Tipu a real opportunity to hone his military skills.

The war was a consequence of the fluid political situation in south India and the competing claims of regional powers in which the British were now involved. Initially, the Marathas and the Nizam of Hyderabad were allied with the British against Haidar, but the Mysore ruler persuaded the Marathas to switch sides. He then gave Tipu his first diplomatic task, sending him, along with two senior *vakils*, including his maternal uncle Ali Reza Khan, Fakhr un-Nissa's brother, to the Hyderabad camp to negotiate a similar change of allegiance with the Nizam. How much Tipu was actually involved in the discussions, given that he was still only sixteen years old, is debatable but the meeting was successfully concluded and he returned triumphantly to his father. This would have been an important formative experience for the young man that he would have continued to build on during the subsequent military actions.

It was at this time that Tipu, in his mid teens, received his first command under the guidance of Ghazi Khan, Ali Reza and a number of other senior officers, and was dispatched to harry the British at Madras. The Mysore contingent reached the outskirts of the town and St Thomas Mount, where they employed themselves in pillaging the country mansions of councillors of the East India Company. Here Tipu observed how the British lived and was fascinated by some of the items they seized from the Europeans, including a microscope he came across in the house of a French merchant. It is likely that this early encounter with Western technologies sparked Tipu's lifelong interest in them. At the same time, Haidar had been engaging the British in South Arcot at Tiruvannamalai, but he suffered a defeat and sent for Tipu and his troops to join him.

Once safely back with his father, Tipu took part in a number of skirmishes before being ordered to the Malabar coast, where a Mysore force was facing strong British opposition. Even though they were successful in taking the town of Mangalore, Tipu's troops failed to secure its fort and it was only when Haidar's larger army arrived to reinforce them that the British retreated, apparently in a disarray of panic. Now on the front foot, Haidar was able to expel the Company's forces from Malabar. But fighting between the two sides continued in the south for another ten months until, at the end of March 1769, Haidar was five miles from Madras. The British sued for peace, a treaty was concluded and prisoners of war exchanged. Territorially, the pre-war situation was reinstated.

Tipu's military training continued virtually uninterrupted, however, as the Marathas invaded Mysore at the end of the same year, with hostilities over disputed territorial claims continuing into mid 1772, when the two sides signed a treaty in which Mysore was forced to cede Gurrumkhonda, Sira, Hoskote, Dodballapur and Kolar, all places with which Haidar and his family had close personal ties. But the death of the Peshwa Madhav Rao in November that same year allowed Haidar to take advantage of the Marathas' ensuing instability, and he sent Tipu to retake all the land Mysore had lost five months earlier. Again Tipu acquitted himself well and he continued to do so over the next few years.

Reading descriptions of Tipu's military actions, one is struck by his fearlessness – never hesitating to plunge into the fray, leading attacks, harrying the enemy, disrupting their supply lines, thinking ahead to outwit his opposition. Yet he was not reckless, knowing when it was wiser to withdraw than continue against intractable odds. And his courage had been evident from an early age, when as a young boy he began to accompany his father on military campaigns. A French mercenary left an account of the steps Haidar took to ensure his son's safety:

> Hyder, who passionately loves his son, and is acquainted with his zeal and courage, was fearful respecting him on account of his very early age; for this reason, he usually entrusted him the

guard of the camp, when he supposed the day would prove too fatiguing or dangerous.

As a result of Tipu's military successes, by the end of 1778, the Mysore realm had reclaimed all its old territory between the Tungabhadra and the Krishna rivers. Haidar was flushed now with victory and on the offensive, his evidently capable eldest son at his side. Nursing his ongoing resentment of British duplicity all those years earlier at Tiruchirappalli, in July 1780 he and Tipu invaded the Carnatic, launching the Second Anglo-Mysore War – the invading army was reported as numbering 90,000.

~

The final step in the making of a prince was a suitable marriage and in 1774 Haidar had decided it was time for Tipu to take a wife. He turned first to his own family connections, the Navayats, and selected the daughter of Imam Sahib Bakhshi from Arcot, a relative of the late Chanda Sahib, a failed candidate for the Nawabship of the Carnatic who had died at the hands of the British. But Haidar faced opposition to this choice from among the women of his court, including Tipu's mother, who suggested instead a lady called Ruqayya Banu, the sister of Burhanuddin Khan, one of Haidar's commanders. It is likely that we see here an example of the competing interests of family members being played out, with Haidar seeking an alliance with his own line and his wife proposing someone from her background. As a compromise, Tipu married both young women at the same time. Five years later, in a purely political arrangement, Haidar married his younger son, Abdul Karim, to the daughter of the Nawab of Savanur (in north-west modern Karnataka), and his daughter Sultan Sahiba to the Nawab's son Abdul Khair Khan. By this time, as we have seen, Haidar had achieved military supremacy in the region and this marriage alliance reflects the changed situation: the Savanur chief had recently submitted to Haidar and the marriages were designed to ensure his loyalty.

Haidar's run of good fortune was not to last, however, and it was during the Second Anglo-Mysore War, in December 1782, that he died, aged about sixty-two, having been ill for some weeks with what is usually described as a carbuncle, suggesting he might have developed blood-poisoning. But before his death he and his son had enjoyed some celebrated victories. After the huge Mysore army had descended the Eastern Ghats into the Carnatic, a number of vigorous battles had taken place, most famously in late 1780 at Pollilur, near Kanchipuram, and in early 1782 at Kumbakonam further south, with the Mysoreans victorious on both occasions, and in mid 1781 at Porto Novo (Parangipettai), where Haidar suffered a defeat. So proud was Tipu of the victory at Pollilur, where he and his father had overcome the Company forces under the command of Colonel John Baillie, that he ordered it commemorated in the famous mural that can still be seen in the Darya Daulat palace at Srirangapattana.

Intended for public viewing, the Darya Daulat mural is made up of two sections, divided by a door, and is 20 metres wide. It reveals in precise detail the different troops involved and the sequence of the battle. It shows Haidar and Tipu on horseback, the French mercenary Lallée, and the square formation of the Madras army, at the centre of which Colonel Baillie sits humiliated (and inaccurately) in a palanquin, a conveyance usually associated with women. The mural's position on the external wall of the palace, although protected from the weather, makes it clear that its purpose was to reinforce Tipu's legitimacy to rule. It is a statement of military power, a visual expression of his successful wielding of the rod of force, the *danda*.

~

When Haidar died, in his camp south-east of Chittoor, close to what is now the southern border of Andhra Pradesh, Tipu was not with him; he was far away in Malabar, where he had been dispatched two months earlier to bolster Mysore forces facing attack by troops of the Company's Bombay army – not an ideal situation in which to secure a smooth succession. We will never know the true details of what occurred immediately following Haidar's death but some reports state that, realising he was dying, Haidar sought the assurance of his senior men that they would stay true to their 'salt' and transfer their allegiance to Tipu. Whatever the case may be, Haidar's death was kept secret to allow time for Tipu to be informed and for his return from Malabar. Haidar's body was apparently concealed in a treasure chest and taken to Kolar, where it was placed in his father's tomb for safe-keeping.

Although a ruler's death is always a vulnerable time for his heir, with threats to his position coming from any quarter keen to profit from the change, there was little opposition to Tipu's taking over from his father. One or two minor conspiracies occurred but the army remained loyal and quickly suppressed them. It took Tipu almost three weeks to reach Haidar's camp but he did so without incident. He formally assumed the title of Nawab Tipu Sultan Bahadur on the evening of 29 December 1782 and seated himself upon the *masnad*. He was now, at the age of thirty-two, in full control of the Mysore realm and its army.

But there was still a war to fight.

3

Consolidation

THE KINGDOM OF MYSORE

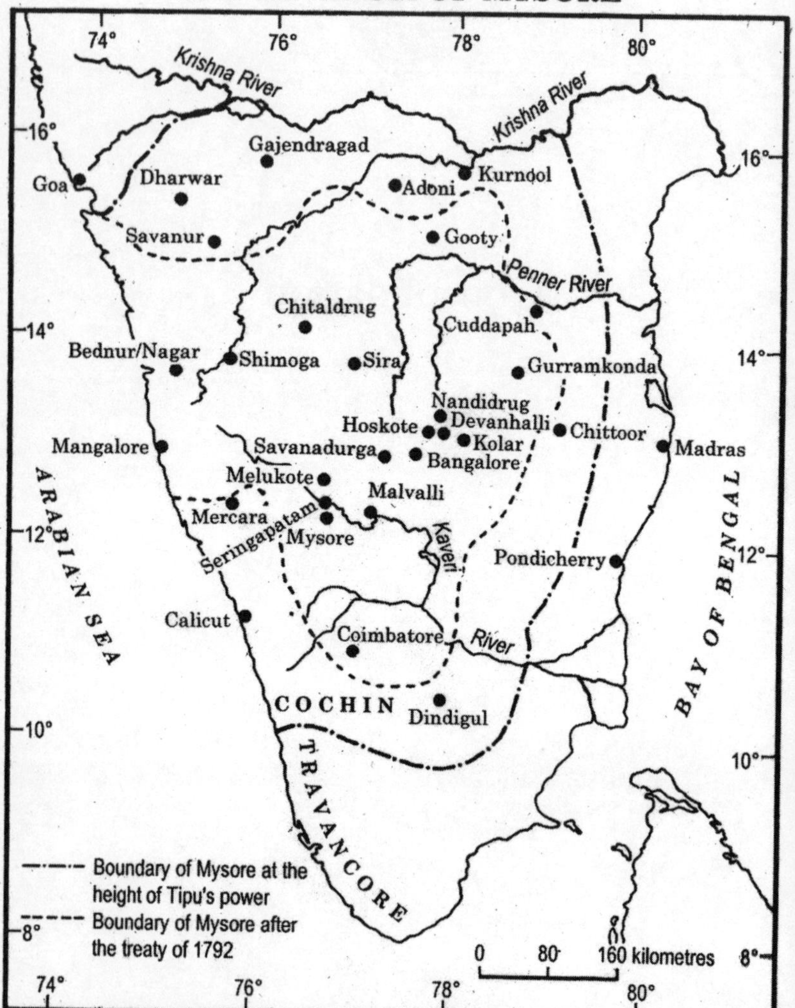

What might Tipu have been thinking as he made his way east towards Chittoor? He has received the probably unexpected news that Haidar has died. He knows that he must travel as quickly as possible, to reach his late father's camp before the fact becomes known outside the inner circle. He is in the company of Maha Mirza Khan, the senior officer dispatched to fetch him and deliver the dreadful message. He has now had time to digest the knowledge that his father has gone, that charismatic man and brilliant soldier who inspired his followers and led them into battle; the central figure in his life whom he has watched since the age of ten become undisputed ruler of the kingdom.

Although Haidar has prepared him to take over, Tipu must feel some trepidation at the size of the boots he has to fill. He and his father were close; he was Haidar's favourite son. Tipu swallows his grief and concentrates solely on the journey ahead. He must reach the camp before the British learn that the bogeyman they have feared for decades is no more. With Maha Mirza Khan's reassurances, he does not doubt that the Mysore army and its officers will remain loyal. He looks into the future: above all, he must prove himself worthy of his inheritance, he must not let his father down. He urges his sure-footed pony onwards. At last, he and Maha Mirza Khan, guarded by a small party of horsemen, plunge down the Eastern Ghats and on to Haidar's camp. Soon, he will be seated in his father's place.

~

Once they had learnt of it, the British recognised the opportunity Haidar's death presented to make headway in the war, but they were late to move in the Carnatic and missed their chance. By February 1783, Tipu and his army had returned to Mysore; the newly installed ruler had unfinished business to attend to in Malabar, where the East India Company's Bombay army was continuing its aggression. Soon news reached him that the British had taken Bednur and he advanced quickly westwards to relieve the town. This he did in April but not in time to stop the emptying of its substantial treasury. The British went on with their hostilities: they seized Mangalore but were then besieged in the fort by Tipu's army. British forces of the Madras army invaded Mysore from the south and made a failed attempt to infiltrate the kingdom from the north-east. The war dragged on until an armistice was agreed in early August, but fighting did not cease completely due to British breaches of the armistice. Eventually, the signing of the Treaty of Mangalore the following April brought almost four years of war to an end.

The terms of the treaty stated that Tipu withdrew all claims to territory in the Carnatic, including Tiruchirappalli, regarded by Haidar as owed to Mysore since the siege in 1751, and the British gave up any idea of placing a Resident at the Mysore court and acquiring the right to conduct trade in the kingdom. They also withdrew their backing for the demands of local chiefs in Kodagu and Malabar to be returned to power. Both sides agreed that neither would support the other's enemies. By now the Company had recognised that the Mysore army was just too big for it to have any hope of defeating it. In addition, its forces were often let down by the inability to keep supply lines open. The treaty was thus a pragmatic agreement between the two opponents. More importantly, it allowed Tipu to embark on the consolidation of his position.

~

Understandably, Tipu's primary goal was to secure and preserve the territory he had inherited from his father. Over the twenty years that Haidar Ali had been in power, he had followed a policy of expanding Mysore's boundaries by reconquering disputed land on the kingdom's borders. He had faced challenges from the British, the Marathas and the Nizam and seized parts of Malabar as well as Kodagu, the area in south Karnataka formerly known as Coorg. Access to Malabar ports was important for trade, as was the control of Bednur, and the incursion into Kodagu was the result of his intervention in a succession dispute at the request of its Raja. Warfare at this time was brutal, and punishment of those who resisted often cruel. It was common practice to set examples to forestall further opposition; this was true of the British, as well as the Indians, although their punishments differed. But what might seem brutal to us must be understood in the light of contemporary practices. The expression 'shock and awe' has been used in recent years to describe military intimidation; it can just as easily be applied to Haidar's and Tipu's treatment of those who rebelled or conspired against them.

Among the punishments Tipu applied to such rebels or conspirators were forced conversion and the transfer of people from their home territories to Mysore, with some of the absent populations replaced by migrants from other regions, such as Bellary district. This was not a religious policy but one of chastisement. The forced removals occurred from both Kodagu and Malabar, the former as a response to continued resistance against Mysore rule, the latter – Nairs and Christians – as a result of their resistance and perceived treachery in the war. The Kanara Christians, in particular, were regarded as inevitable 'fellow-travellers' of the British because of their shared faith. Forced conversion would lead to the loss of caste, and thus community, but if a person was prepared to convert willingly he would receive better treatment and be employed within Mysore itself. A section of the Mysore army was made up of *chelas* or 'slave' troops. Known by various appellations, including *asad-i ilahi*, they were captives, both European and Indian, who were coerced into service as soldiers after converting to Islam, either willingly or through force. The loyalty of these men could not be relied upon, however, and they were administered separately from the regular Mysore troops; they would frequently desert when an opportunity arose.

During the remaining years of the 1780s, then, Tipu dealt with the consequences of both Haidar's death and the recent war, which had provided encouragement to those who wished to break free from Mysore or recapture disputed territory. It was during this period that the forced transfers occurred from Kodagu, whose chiefs continued to rebel, ultimately retaking and holding all their territory in early 1788, except for the fort of Mercara. And in 1788–89 Tipu suppressed a conspiracy against him involving his brother-in-law Abdul Khair Khan of Savanur. In late 1786, the Marathas again invaded from the north, but within months they had suffered defeats and setbacks, until peace terms were agreed in April 1787 at Gajendragad. Yet despite these distractions, up until the start of the Third Anglo-Mysore War in 1790, Tipu devoted a large part of his energy to building on Haidar's legacy. He did this within the parameters of recognised notions of Indian kingship but in his own and often innovative way.

~

Authority to hold power on the subcontinent derived from the figure of the Mughal emperor and lip-service to this convention continued to be paid right up until the overthrow of Bahadur Shah II in 1858. Even the British relied on Mughal *sanads*, written edicts, to legitimate their appropriation of territory and the income it provided. The Wodeyars and other south Indian dynasties also had sought Mughal sanction for their rule. It was one thing to hold de facto power but it was another to hold it legally, so it was to this matter that Tipu now turned his attention.

Having made the decision to discard the pretence that he ruled in the name of the Wodeyars, it was necessary that Tipu find an alternative source of juristic authority. To this end, he asked the French, with whom he had lines of communication, to approach the Mughal emperor Shah Alam to secure a *sanad* on his behalf. But the British lobbied hard against the request. As a result, the emperor refused, instead granting Tipu an impressive title, 'Umdat ul-Mulk Mubarak ud-Daulat Tipu Sultan Fath Ali Khan Bahadur Hizabr Jang Fadwi Shah Alam Badshah Ghazi', that accorded him the status of warlike hero but underlined his subordination to the Badshah. Under different circumstances, Tipu might have seen this outcome as a setback but, always the pragmatist and knowing that he could challenge the enfeebled emperor without fear of retribution, he set about asserting his legitimacy through other means.

Within Mysore, this process took the form first of issuing coins – at the height of Tipu's power the kingdom boasted eleven mints. In a departure from the approach taken by Haidar, Tipu's higher denomination coins, those in gold and silver, carried a *julus* or reign year, a very public declaration of kingship. Pointedly, unlike other Indian rulers of the time, none of his coins made reference to the Mughal emperor or to his *julus*. Many of the coins also carried the image of an elephant, an obviously royal reference. Secondly, in an overt statement of independence, Tipu ordered that his own name and not that of Shah Alam be inserted in the *khutba*, the Friday sermon delivered in all mosques throughout the realm. For centuries, this practice had been the primary means adopted by Muslim rulers to express their legitimacy. It could only be done with the support of the *'ulama* and was an open acknowledgement of the king's right to rule. There appears to have been little opposition to this order. If questioned,

Tipu cited religious authority for the change – clearly, at least on this issue, Haidar's education of his son had not been wasted.

More controversial, though, was Tipu's adoption in 1786 of the royal title *badshah* – a direct challenge to Shah Alam. To take one of the emperor's titles as his own was a presumption of the highest order. Again, this was only possible in the light of Shah Alam's weakened status. Inside his realm, Tipu could take such a step with ease, since he was the final arbiter on such things, but outside Mysore his right to use the title, unsurprisingly, was not accepted. During negotiations at Gajendragad in 1787, for example, the Marathas insisted that he merely be referred to as Nawab Tipu Sultan Fath Ali Khan, a point they ultimately won. But Tipu was not deterred. Instead, he looked abroad for acknowledgement of his status.

~

A particular feature of the Muslim world is its interconnectedness. By the eighteenth century, Islam had spread far and wide, adopting many local characteristics as it did so but maintaining the over-arching concept of the *ummah*, the broader Muslim community. What welded the *ummah* together was the Hajj, the pilgrimage to Mecca required of all able-bodied Muslims at least once in their lifetime. Naturally, for a range of reasons – often financial – many Muslims are unable to make the journey, especially if they live in distant lands. Even so, the requirement and undertaking of the Hajj, as well as Islam's history as a faith of merchants and sailors, meant that Tipu's view of the world was not insular, it was one that looked outwards, beyond the confines of the subcontinent, a view that was bolstered by the growing European presence in the region.

In November 1785, a large contingent from Mysore, comprising troops, servants, officials and four *vakils*, left Srirangapattana for the port of Tadri on the Malabar coast. They were charged with a mission from Tipu to the Ottoman Sultan Abdul Hamid I in Istanbul. The embassy, under the leadership of Ghulam Ali Khan, carried detailed instructions, along with a huge array of gifts – many of local manufacture – spices, textiles, jewellery and gold and silver coins. In early March 1786, the travellers set sail in four ships for Muscat; also on board were four elephants – three intended as gifts and one to be sold to raise funds for the mission's return. Sadly, none of the unfortunate creatures survived the voyage.

Mysore already had an agent and warehouse in Muscat and part of the purpose of the embassy was commercial. There was also a religious aspect to the journey, requiring the *vakils* to present gifts at any holy sites that they visited. And finally, they were to convey Tipu's requests to Abdul Hamid, who was still regarded by many in the Muslim world – due to his guardianship of Mecca and Medina – as Caliph. As well as seeking Ottoman assistance in combating the rise of British power,

Tipu sought the Sultan's confirmation, as Caliph, of the legitimacy of his claim to rule Mysore. It was to be four years before the *vakils* returned with Abdul Hamid's approval – not that Tipu waited for the Sultan's imprimatur before proclaiming himself *badshah*, but its receipt certainly would have reinforced his right to do so.

In approaching the Ottoman Sultan in this way, Tipu was conforming to the practice of earlier Muslim rulers in India, who prior to the ascendancy of the Mughals had themselves turned to the Ottoman Caliph to legitimate their rule. However, when planning the embassy, Tipu had also considered having the *vakils* continue on to France and to England. In the end he decided against it, for which the four men undoubtedly thanked him once they were under way. Their journey was arduous and often hazardous, with many men and three of the Mysore ships lost by the time they reached Basra. Instead, in July 1787, Tipu dispatched a separate embassy to France. Although this later embassy lacked the religious element, both missions demonstrate the breadth of Tipu's vision for Mysore.

~

As with the British, the French too had involved themselves in the regional politics of the south. The competition and sometimes enmity between the two countries meant that both Haidar and Tipu regarded the French as their ally and French mercenaries were an important component of the Mysore army. In 1779, the mercenary Lallée had left the Nizam's employ to join Haidar, bringing with him a substantial number of soldiers; the Frenchman fought in many actions alongside Tipu and continued to serve him after Haidar's death. But the strength of the friendship between the two powers did fluctuate, and during the 1780s Tipu felt that the French at Pondicherry were no longer as supportive as they had been previously. He was disappointed that despite their promises French involvement in the Second Anglo-Mysore

War had been lukewarm at best. In an attempt to improve relations, Tipu decided instead to deal directly with his French counterpart, Louis XVI, the king who would later lose his head to the guillotine in the French Revolution.

Although this second embassy ultimately failed in its objective of securing an offensive and defensive treaty with the French government, to stall British expansion on the subcontinent, it was more successful in acquiring the items and men that Tipu had requested. These included gunsmiths, bomb-makers, watchmakers, workers of porcelain from Sèvres, glass-workers, textile-weavers, printers who could work with Eastern languages, an engineer and a physician. Many plants too were on the list, not all of which grew in France: clove and camphor trees, European fruit trees, seeds of various flowers and linseed. Tipu's goal was to match the Europeans in their technology and industry, which would set Mysore apart and stimulate the prosperity of the realm;

just as he wished to compete with the British militarily, he wanted to match their economic enterprise.

~

Mysore already had a wealth of natural and manufacturing resources, providing Tipu with a substantial foundation for his economic expansion and commercial developments. In the mid 1780s, French officials at Pondicherry had sent an economic and military review of the kingdom to their government in Paris. It survives in the French National Archives to this day. The review listed natural resources as:

> pepper, sandalwood, cardamom, cotton textiles, rice, other grains and lacquer; its expansive forests offer products for the maritime powers: leather, coir, iron, ink, muslin, and voiles which are manufactured there.

In terms of Mysore's military capability, the officials noted that:

> At Seringapatam, where they manufacture ten muskets per day, there are ammunition depots; also at Bangalore and Nagar [Bednur] where they prepare ammunition for their artillery. The Nawab also has foundries in these places for the manufacture of bronze cannons. There are gold mines in this country in the ranges of Coorg; the rivers carry gold grains sometimes as big as a pepper pea.

Both Haidar and Tipu were energetic in their ambitions for Mysore. Recognising that the nature of commerce in the eighteenth century was essentially maritime, Haidar had begun to develop a navy; he also reformed the army along European lines, abolishing the system of *jagirs*, the link between land assignments and military service. He and Tipu streamlined revenue collection, cutting out the involvement of middlemen, and in the late

1780s Tipu made further administrative changes, such as dividing the kingdom into eighteen divisions. He embarked on an extensive building programme – roads, mosques, administrative buildings, the repair of forts – and established new market towns. He issued regulations far and wide.

Tipu's day was always full and regularly ordered. When not campaigning or travelling his realm, he resided at his capital on Srirangapattana, either in his main palace within the fort or in the two smaller palaces of the Darya Daulat Bagh, in the middle of the island, and the Lal Bagh, near Haidar's tomb. He began his day with ablutions and prayers, followed by some exercise and a light breakfast. Then he would consult with his officials, issue instructions and dictate correspondence. This was followed by a meeting with his astrologers and physicians, in order to ascertain the state of his health. At this time, Tipu would also inspect the fresh flowers, fruit and vegetables brought to him daily from the numerous gardens in his realm. He would reserve the best for the palace kitchens and the women's quarters and send the remainder to be sold in the local market. At around 9 a.m. he shared a larger meal with some of his senior men and two or three of his sons.

After dining, dressed in his finery – turban with jewelled ornament, pearl necklaces and rings, as well as, unusually, a European pocket watch hanging from a fob – Tipu would proceed to the public audience hall, where he would hold his formal darbar. The darbar conformed to those of other Indian kings and was highly ritualised, with rigid protocol and clearly defined roles for participants. Here petitions were presented and people seeking favour made their obeisance. The heads of the government's different departments made their reports and requests. Tipu would then receive his post master, who would deliver any letters that had come from across the kingdom, as well as from Mysore's agents at other courts and from other rulers or their agents.

It was also in the darbar that Tipu ruled on the punishment of miscreants – the more gruesome penalties could include the slicing off of ears or noses, as well as whipping. The darbar ended at about 3 p.m., when Tipu would retire to take a nap for an hour, after which he would perform his regulatory prayers. His religious duties completed, he then left the palace, sometimes to review his troops, at other times to inspect his cannon and musket foundries, or any building projects that might be under way. Because of his close interest in and encouragement of local manufactures, such as textiles, Tipu would occasionally inspect those also. About an hour after sunset he rode back to his palace, most likely to spend the rest of the evening with his family.

~

It was through Haidar's efforts that Mysore's boundaries had expanded, and Tipu, as his heir, was charged with not only holding on to that territory but also continuing and refining his father's administrative and commercial agenda.

In order to achieve this, it was essential that he consolidate his position in the face of the many challenges that confronted him, not least the external pressures from the competing powers of Hyderabad, the Marathas and the British. As the 1780s progressed, and he resolved his dispute with the Marathas and dispatched his embassies to Istanbul and France, there would have seemed little reason to turn from that path. But fortune had other plans for him. In 1790 a border dispute with the Travancore Raja led to the outbreak of the Third Anglo-Mysore War. When in April of that year Tipu stormed the defensive barrier known as the Travancore lines, he triggered a response that would change his life forever.

4

Broken Dreams

While Tipu had been pushing ahead with his reforms within Mysore and consolidating his position, outside the kingdom the political meddling of the British continued. Although they were constrained by the Treaty of Mangalore from taking direct offensive action against Tipu, in a bid to weaken him they encouraged the ambitions of the Marathas and the Nizam. Both these powers resented the territories lost to Mysore and were keen to obtain the Company's assistance in regaining them. In 1786 a new governor-general was appointed. Earl Cornwallis, who had served as a lieutenant-general during the American Revolution and, due to his surrender at Yorktown in 1781, was regarded by many as responsible for the loss of the American colonies, took up the post. Based in Calcutta, the governor-general oversaw the political affairs of the East India Company's possessions in Bengal, Bombay and Madras. The American defeat had tarnished Cornwallis's reputation and he was keen to restore it. Despite instructions to maintain a non-offensive approach, he worked behind the scenes to destabilise Tipu, whom he regarded as the greatest barrier to the growth of British commerce and influence on the subcontinent. The governor-general saw Tipu as

> a prince of very uncommon ability and of boundless ambition, who had acquired a degree of power in extent of territory, in wealth, and in forces that threatened the Company's possessions in the Carnatic and those of all his other neighbours with imminent danger.

Although the first part of Cornwallis's statement was an accurate assessment of Tipu's wealth and abilities, the conclusion that he was an 'imminent danger' to his neighbours, including themselves, was an exaggeration. Unlike the British, Tipu regarded the treaties he signed as binding; in contrast, British involvement in local politics, and their intriguing with those who held a grudge against him, frequently broke the spirit, and at times the terms, of the treaty they had agreed with him. One of the malcontents with whom they aligned themselves was the Raja of Travancore, Rama Varma, whose territory covered what is now the southern half of Kerala round to Kanyakumari in Tamil Nadu.

Rama Varma had harboured resentments against Mysore since he had fallen out with Haidar in the 1760s. The defensive lines he had constructed in 1764 ran from east to west to protect from invasion an exposed part of Travancore's northern border. Made up of a huge ditch, ramparts and a thick bamboo hedge, a portion of the lines ran through Cochin (Kochi) – in the 1780s, territory under the control of Mysore.

Tipu asked Rama Varma to demolish the barrier as it was blocking access to a large part of Cochin. Rama Varma refused. The Raja was also providing refuge to several Malabar chiefs who did not wish to submit to Mysore. Again, when Tipu asked him to hand over the men, the Raja refused. He then provoked Tipu further by purchasing two coastal islands from the Dutch, islands that Tipu himself had wished to buy.

The diplomatic approach having failed, in an attempt to change the Raja's mind Tipu then tried military intimidation, marching with a force towards the lines in December 1789. Some skirmishes broke out between Mysore and Travancore troops but Tipu did not attack, preferring to resolve the issue through negotiation. Increasingly, though, his troops faced assaults from Travancore, whose soldiers would launch raids on them from inside their territory. Not surprisingly, the Mysore troops fought back. Realising there was now no hope of securing a peaceful resolution, Tipu decided to invade. In early April 1790, he forced a breach in the lines with a cannonade. The British, allied with Travancore and looking for a reason to attack Tipu, declared war on him. It is not clear if Tipu had anticipated this response to his actions but the Mysore ruler first tried to negotiate a solution, asking that he might send *vakils* to the British authorities in Madras, but Cornwallis was adamant that the time for a peaceful resolution was over. The governor-general knew that he held the upper hand: there was a good chance of securing the support of the Marathas and the Nizam, as well as a number of the Malabar chiefs, and there was no chance of the French coming to Tipu's aid – back in Europe, the French Revolution was in full swing.

Over the next few months, Cornwallis signed treaties with the Nizam and the Marathas, the Rajas of Kodagu and Cochin, the Bibi of Cannanore, the Mapilla ruler of the small coastal state centred on Kannur – the Bibi reluctantly, as only the previous year, in a political alliance, her daughter had married one of Tipu's sons –

and several other Malabar chiefs. The British also entered into negotiations with the Wodeyar Dowager Rani, the determined Lakshmi Ammani, who was continuing her campaign to reinstate her family to power. Initially, when Tipu invaded the Carnatic towards the end of the year, he enjoyed some victories, but in December 1790 his forces suffered defeat in Malabar, which established British supremacy in the area. Then something unprecedented happened.

The following February, Cornwallis led his army into Mysore itself and in March captured the prized city of Bangalore; by May he was within a few miles of Srirangapattana. But, in a reprieve for Tipu, the climate and the usual British problem of unreliable supplies meant that before the end of the month the enemy had to return to Bangalore. Cornwallis had been awaiting allied Maratha and Hyderabad troops as reinforcements but their late arrival, combined with lack of food, sickness among his men, and the imminent onset of the monsoon, led to his tactical retreat. Earlier, in April, after a long siege, the Marathas had taken the northern fort of Dharwar from Tipu, but that victory was nothing compared to the blow Cornwallis struck with his invasion of Mysore's heartland.

The British remained in Bangalore through the period of the rains and then restarted their offensive, supported by their Hyderabad and Maratha allies. Further Mysore forts fell and in February 1792 British troops attacked Srirangapattana. Less than three weeks later, Tipu was ready to discuss peace. On 24 February, preliminaries of peace were settled and work began on negotiating a treaty, eventually signed on 18 March.

The treaty was crushing for Tipu. It required him to pay an indemnity of 3 crore rupees plus 30 lakh rupees, in what were euphemistically referred to as 'durbar charges' – in effect, gifts to the allied commanders. Mysore also lost almost half of its territory, with Hyderabad and the Marathas retaking land on which they had claims, and the British acquiring land they had not previously held:

Baramahal and Dindigul districts, all of Kodagu and a large section of the Malabar coast, including Calicut (Kozhikode) and Cannanore. To ensure that he met the terms of the treaty, the British forced Tipu to give up two of his sons as hostages; Abdul Khaliq, who was eight, and Muizuddin, aged five, were handed over to Cornwallis. The boys were not alone, however – Tipu's senior *vakil*, Ghulam Ali Khan, and his uncle, Ali Reza Khan, remained with them throughout the two years they were held in Madras. Even though they were captives, the princes were treated well, as befitted their status, and entertained in local society – they would have been something of a curiosity to the European inhabitants of the town – but they had left behind a distraught family, whose anguish had delayed the children's departure.

~

Let us pause for a moment and consider from Tipu's viewpoint the events of the previous two years. At the start of 1790, he had ruled a kingdom that stretched south from Dharwar and the river Krishna to beyond Dindigul; to the west his control had extended as far as the coast and in the east to the border of the Carnatic (see map on page 40). Mysore itself was fertile and prosperous; agriculture and industry flourished. The population of the capital Srirangapattana is believed to have numbered more than 100,000, its inhabitants employed in supporting the government and the court. Now Tipu found himself facing a crippling debt and a great part of the territory he had inherited from Haidar was lost, which in turn made the huge sum all the more difficult to pay – and, until he discharged the debt, two of his sons would remain in the hands of the British. How might you respond to such a reversal in fortune? If you were an adherent of the Muslim faith, as was Tipu, you might well see the hand of God in such disaster.

No doubt, following the handover of his sons, Tipu had time to reflect on what had happened.

Could his own actions have led to this calamity? What might he have done to prevent it? And the big question – had he offended God in some way? Possibly he discussed such issues with his closest confidants, perhaps with family members. We cannot know. What is clear, though, is that from 1792 onward his reign became more Islamic in character. Up until then, Tipu had always referred to his government as the *sarkar-i haidari*, emphasising his inheritance from Haidar; from now on it was to be the *sarkar-i khudadadi*, the God-given realm. He now understood his conflict with the British as a *jihad*, or at least desired to portray it as such – being Christian, they were a prime target for such rhetoric. He ordered the composition of *khutbas*, sermons, on the merits of *jihad*, *'ilm* (religious learning) and prayer, and instructed the Qazi of Srirangapattana to compose a treatise on the duties of Muslims, with an emphasis on *jihad*. He commissioned works on hadiths and the Qur'an.

Initially, Tipu concentrated on the repayment

of the debt and the return of his sons, which occurred in March 1794, but then he redoubled his efforts to raise support for the expulsion of the British from India. He wrote to potential allies far and wide: the Nizam, the Afghan ruler Zaman Shah, the Ottoman Sultan Selim III, as well as the French. No help was forthcoming. After Tipu's death, Lord Mornington's supporters would use this correspondence as justification for the final attack on Mysore. Increasingly desperate, Tipu was prepared to clutch at any hope that might present itself. In late 1797, a Frenchman of dubious origin, an adventurer who had recently arrived at Srirangapattana, deceived Tipu into believing that he came as an emissary from the French colony of Mauritius. He persuaded Tipu to dispatch an embassy to the island, to ask the French governor to raise an expeditionary force to come to Mysore's aid. Against the advice of a number of his senior men, Tipu went ahead with the plan. It was to result in his downfall.

The governor of Mauritius, a man named

Malartic, puzzled by the Mysore embassy's request and unable to provide the required troops, issued a proclamation in January 1798. It was a bid to raise troops from among the island's inhabitants and it set out Tipu's aims. The purpose of this until now secret Mysore mission was suddenly public knowledge. In June, the Mauritius governor's announcement appeared in a Calcutta newspaper and the British saw their opportunity. Lord Mornington, who had taken up the post of governor-general in 1797, ordered the Madras army mobilised in preparation for war. A few months later, the Nizam signed a treaty that reduced Hyderabad to a British subsidiary.

Learning of these aggressive actions, Tipu attempted to negotiate. Lord Mornington, though, was not for turning – a man of imperial ambition, he was determined to force Tipu's capitulation. The outcome is well known: on 4 May 1799, Tipu died after British troops attacked Srirangapattana and breached the fort. The most credible account of his death, based on information supplied by those who were there, is that he had gone out of his palace to investigate a report that one of his generals had been killed. But by this time, enemy soldiers had entered the fort through the breach and Tipu joined in the defence. He fell, wounded. In the melee, as he lay where his men had placed him, a British soldier tried to remove his jewelled belt. Attempting to stop him, Tipu struck out with the sword he still held in his hand. The soldier shot him.

~

Among the many items the British found in the palace at Srirangapattana in 1799 was a book containing a record of Tipu's dreams, written in his own hand. Until recently, the *khwab-nama*, now held in the British Library in London, was regarded more as a curiosity than having much historical value. The dreams themselves, thirty-seven in all, date from April 1786 to 16 January 1799, leading historians to believe that the book was compiled over that entire period. But close analysis of its content has now revealed that the register is instead directly connected to the final years of Tipu's life and that it dates from no earlier than 1795.

The following is an extract from the first dream in the register, which Tipu records as having occurred in the early hours of 6 April 1786:

> The Maratha army had arrived and I was throwing out a challenge to its commander to come forward and fight singly. A Muslim officer, who was their accomplice, accepted the challenge. In the battlefield, while both armies were facing each other, by the grace of God I fought alone, I killed the idolater who was the unbelievers' accomplice with one single strike of the sword. Thereupon the commander of the army, who was a youth, fled.

Of the later dreams, two from 7 June 1798 make an interesting contrast. Tipu experienced one in the afternoon of that day, presumably while taking his nap, and the other during the night. They appear to have nothing in common but he recorded them both. In the first, he writes how he dreamt he had gone into a garden with several buildings – he had been told that the famous fifteenth-century Persian poet Jami was there.

> I went to the Maulana [Jami] and expressed my pleasure at his arrival. The Maulana said to me, 'I have come to meet you'. I again repeated how nice and appropriate it was that he had come, and added, 'In olden times lived Maulana Sa'di, and, in our own, God Almighty had produced Maulana Jami and sent him to us. I shall seek his blessings'. Having said that I took the Maulana with me to my residence.

The second dream has an altogether different tone:

> That very night, in the early hours of the morning I had another dream: A young and

beautiful woman, putting on costly jewellery and clothes, came to me. She was carrying three ripe plantain fruits of the size of large cucumbers. She handed over the fruits to this servant of God, and I said I had never seen such plantain fruit. I ate one of them and found it extremely sweet and delicious. In the meantime, I woke up.

The content of the *khwab-nama*, then, is 'dreamlike' in that the dreams have that quality of the fantastical, as well as the pragmatic and bizarre, and Tipu's recording of these dreams and not others tells us that for him they were significant, although we cannot always tell *why* he thought this. For us, however, it is the register's structure and the dates of the dreams that are most informative. It seems that Tipu was compiling the book with a specific purpose, as part of the wider arsenal of divinatory practices available to him, such as astrology and bibliomancy (opening books at random, usually the Qur'an or the *Diwan* of Hafiz). By recording earlier dreams, from the period of his greatest military successes in the 1780s, and noting significant events and dreams that occurred in the present from the mid 1790s, Tipu was taking a practical approach to interpreting, managing and perhaps even influencing the difficult situation in which he found himself.

It was not at all uncommon for Muslim kings to engage in such activity. There is a long tradition of dream interpretation in Islam, known as *ta'bir* and regarded as a science. The practice is based in an understanding of the world that makes no distinction between the spiritual and the material, a concept familiar to followers of most Eastern faiths. In Islam, there is the notion of the 'unseen realm', *'alam ul-ghalib*, a supranormal or 'other' reality. An aspect of this supranormal reality is the *'alam ul-mithal*, the 'imaginal world', which mystics regard as the realm where what is to come takes shape. For Muslims, dreams and visions provide access to this world and are therefore predictive. One can only know, though, whether a dream has accurately foretold the future by looking to the past, after what was predicted has (or has not) happened. So this is why Tipu went back to his dreams of the 1780s, perhaps already recorded elsewhere: by comparing the dreams he was experiencing with those that occurred earlier, when he was at the height of his powers, he hoped better to understand his present. In doing so, he might then be able to take effective steps to ameliorate the declining circumstances that he faced.

The fact that the *khwab-nama* dates from the mid 1790s places it firmly in the period when Tipu was doing his utmost to rally support amongst potential allies. In 1795, with his sons finally back in the bosom of the family, it is possible that he had regained a certain optimism. The register's compilation therefore is unlikely to have been an act of desperation but rather part of a range of strategies he adopted to counteract the creeping influence of the British and to avoid further setbacks. How he went about dealing with his difficulties was a direct result of his education as a youth. Well-versed in Islamic scholarship, history and mysticism – the last most likely through his reading of the great Sufi poets – he had the tools with which to counteract his decline in fortune.

Earlier writers on Tipu failed to recognise the significance of his dream register because they ignored the historical and cultural context of its production. That they did so should serve as a reminder of the perils of such an approach. As we have seen, Tipu was a son of south India, as was his father; he was steeped in the cultural and regional environment of his time. We must consider, therefore, the nature of the milieu on which he drew, both to express the character of his rule and to convey his awesome power – the milieu to which he spoke.

Portrait of Tipu Sultan, gouache. Anonymous Indian artist, Mysore, c. 1790–1800.
Pictures from History/Bridgeman Images.

Previous page: Tipu Sultan on an Elephant, detail from 'The Battle of Pollilur' mural, Darya Daulat Palace, Srirangapattana, babri (tiger stripe) decoration visible on elephant's cloth, howdah and parasol. Mysore, 1784. Pictures from History/Bridgeman Images.

Above: 'Tipu's Tiger', Mysore, c. 1790–92 (wood). Tipu's famous mechanical tiger has a miniature organ with keyboard and bellows to simulate the groans of a dying British officer. Victoria & Albert Museum, London, UK/Bridgeman Images.

verleaf, top: The hilt of a sword seized after the fall of Srirangapattana, with tiger's head pommel and ms set in the babri (tiger stripe) pattern. Mysore, c. 1787–93. Pictures from History/Bridgeman Images.

verleaf, bottom: An embroidered quiver, (with seven arrows) arm guards and belt, all with babri ger stripe) decoration, taken after the fall of Srirangapattana. Mysore, c. 1787–93. Pictures from istory/Bridgeman Images.

Previous page, top: Tipu delivers to Ghulam Ali Khan his two sons, who in turn bid farewell to an older brother. Although imaginary, this moving depiction of the hostage princes, prior to their handover to Lord Cornwallis and their departure from Srirangapattana, conveys the family's emotion. Mezzotint, British schoo engraver: Jospeh Grozer (c. 1755–98). © The British Library Board.

Previous page, bottom: An example of the propagandist paintings produced in Britain after Tipu's death to celebrate his killing and glorify the capture of Srirangapattana. Artist: Henry Singleton (1766–1839).

Above: The Gumbaz, the tomb of Haidar Ali and Tipu Sultan, post-1799, showing British troops in the grounds. Hand-coloured engraving, published 1806; original artist: Charles Gold. The Stapleton Collection/Bridgeman Images.

5

Matters of Faith

There is more than a little truth in the statement 'The past is a foreign country; they do things differently there', the famous opening sentence of L.P. Hartley's novel *The Go-Between*. And the more distant the past, the more foreign it can appear. Looking back to the eighteenth century, not so very distant when compared to the preceding millennia of recorded history, it can seem that life was not so unlike our own. Collective memories of Tipu Sultan, either positive or negative, persist amongst a number of populations in south India, such as the Nairs and the Kanara Christians, as well as the inhabitants of Karnataka generally. And the presence of Europeans on the subcontinent for over 200 years allowed Indians, in both the north and the south, to become accustomed (if not reconciled) to such foreigners. Consequently, the reader might feel – mistakenly – that there is a kind of familiarity to the period in which Tipu lived.

Earlier, we considered what it might have been like to have been alive at that time; we saw that for many Indians their world had yet to experience the economic and social disruption that followed the establishment of the British Raj. Certainly, it is the case that on the coasts, where European trading companies were active, and the occasional Christian missionary disembarked in the hope of 'saving souls', local people were beginning to experience some of the change that came only later to inland communities. In Haidar and Tipu's Mysore, though, life continued unaffected; the society remained very much one of warriors, merchants and peasants – plus an admixture of priests, holy men and pirs – and people still understood the local rhetoric of kingship and power. For Tipu, wishing to portray himself as the Badshah and rightful ruler of the realm, it was to just such rhetoric that he turned.

~

The most well-known image associated with Tipu is that of the tiger. After he died, it became his epithet – 'the Tiger of Mysore' the British called him. Tipu's use of tiger imagery – either a stylised tiger stripe, known as *babri*, or a representation of an actual tiger, usually just the head – was designed to convey his awesome power and demonstrate his close connection with the divine. The motif appeared most magnificently on his gold and jewel-encrusted throne but also on flags and banners, on *chubs* or staffs, on soldiers' uniforms, on coins, on Tipu's own clothing, as wall decoration, as brands on animals, on weapons – swords, muskets and cannons – on seals, on the leather binding of books and on fabric used as canopies or wall hangings, as well as on the howdahs and related furnishings of the royal elephants. It was even used as a watermark on paper. Among the loot taken from Srirangapattana was an elaborate betel dish of pierced silver, decorated with *babri* in relief; it most likely formed part of a full betel service for use in court ceremonial. Thus the tiger was everywhere. Yet it was not the only visual expression of Tipu's rule: almost as prevalent was solar imagery, often combined with the *babri* stripe to represent the sun's rays. The British emphasis of the tiger over the sun tells us more about them than it does about their victim. To the British, the tiger was the counterpoint to their lion; it made sense to them in that context. But it was not Europeans who were Tipu's intended audience.

In the cultural milieu in which Tipu lived both the tiger and the sun emblems carried a range of symbolic meanings, depending upon the observer. As a Muslim ruler of predominantly non-Muslim subjects, it was essential that Tipu draw upon imagery that resonated with all communities. Furthermore, in eighteenth-century south India, the region's different religious groups were less divided than they might appear today. As already noted, this was a non-modern world, unaffected by Enlightenment notions of rational thought, where people engaged with the spiritual world through common sacred sites and practices. There was an overlap in the way that local Muslims and non-Muslims regarded the worlds of gods and pirs, an overlap that featured strong warrior elements grounded within a common sacred geography. People followed their own deities and spiritual heroes but in a way that would have been recognisable to members of local communities other than their own.

Let us first consider the significance of the sun motif. For millennia, Indian kings had claimed descent from either the sun or the moon and many adopted the practice of showing themselves to their subjects at dawn, in imitation of the rising sun, so that the people below could receive *darshan*. So ingrained was the practice, several of the Mughal emperors are known also to have followed it, appearing every morning at sunrise on a palace balcony. And while this association of the sun and its rays with Indian kings has great antiquity, Muslims could understand it in the context of *nur*, God's light, the divine essence. As a result of the close relationship between divine and royal power, therefore, all kings in India, whatever their religious affiliation, were regarded as radiating a kind of divine energy or light. The most common epithet used to refer to Tipu in the Persian sources is *huzur-i pur-i nur*, which is usually translated as 'the Resplendent Presence', indicating how central the solar imagery was to his self-perception. A further influence on Tipu might have been a local history of sun worship in Mysore, which had later become linked with regional 'sun' goddesses. Tipu probably would not have been able to articulate quite so clearly what lay behind his use of the sun emblem, but he would have known with certainty that it was recognisably royal to each and every one of his subjects.

Similar processes were at work in Tipu's

adoption of the tiger symbol, with the sole difference that, although Haidar had also used solar imagery, the tiger was Tipu's innovation. And what an innovation it was. Not so much the tiger itself but the way that he used it: it would have been impossible to be in Tipu's vicinity or in the vicinity of his troops and not be surrounded by tiger imagery. It was, if you like, unavoidable, with certain features, especially the use of the *babri* stripe in decoration, uniquely his. The observer would have been in no doubt that they were witness to an emphatic statement.

Tipu's adoption of the tiger as his emblem again had its roots in the local cultural environment. The green velvet banner on display at Windsor Castle, with its calligraphic tiger mask, tells us a great deal about how the tiger image carried meaning for Muslim and non-Muslim alike. The epithet 'Victorious Lion of God' refers to Imam Ali, the Prophet's cousin and son-in-law, the fourth Rightly Guided Caliph, who for Muslims is the archetypal warrior. Ali is also regarded as the originator of all Sufi orders apart from the Naqshbandiyyas and, for Shi'as, the true successor to Muhammad. Another of Ali's epithets is 'Haidar', which within India can mean either 'lion' or 'tiger'. And it is this linguistic inter-changeability of 'tiger' and 'lion' on the subcontinent that allows the conflation of the tiger mask and the epithet 'Victorious Lion of God': in India *asad allah ul-ghalib*, 'victorious lion of God', could also mean 'victorious tiger of God'.

In contrast, for non-Muslim south Indians, the tiger has close associations not only with royalty but also with warrior goddesses who ride tigers (as do at times warrior pirs). In certain contexts, the tiger represents *shakti*, divine female energy that is considered dangerous; it has been argued that Shiva wears a tiger skin to signify his control of *shakti*. Historically, tiger skins had also featured as part of royal regalia – Shivaji, for example, sat upon a tiger-skin seat. More specifically, in Tipu's case, the use of the tiger motif distinguished his rule from that of the Wodeyars, whose emblems were the double-headed bird, the *gandabherunda*, and the boar. Instead, it carried echoes of earlier dynasties who had used tiger imagery, such as the Cholas, the Sindas and the Hoysalas.

Tipu was culturally immersed in the only world he knew. As Haidar's successor, he was determined to create a strong dynasty with a strong visual identity – we should not forget that many of his subjects would have been illiterate and the only way to convey such a message would have been visually. Throughout history, and not just on the subcontinent, kings have used display to overawe, usually combined with religious language and symbolism to bolster their legitimacy. It is no coincidence that Louis XIV of France was known as the Sun King, nor that European monarchs claimed the 'divine right' to rule. In Tipu's case, the sun and the tiger had both regional and broader Islamic associations, making them effective markers of his kingship for Muslims and non-Muslims alike. When the royal progress left Srirangapattana fort – passing through the elephant gate, banners flying, troops marching or riding in front and behind, Tipu's emblems decorating objects, animals and men – no one who saw it would have questioned for a moment that here was the procession of a king.

~

It was also important, if Tipu were to retain power, that he tap into the south's shared sacred landscape, and it is in this light that we should read his patronage of religious institutions, which was widespread. For centuries, kings had associated themselves with the sacred sites of the region, the most significant being the river Kaveri, the Ganges of the south. Rising in the hills of Kodagu, the river wends its way across the Mysore plateau and down onto the plains of Tamil Nadu. Its entire length is dotted with religious landmarks, small and large. For south Indian kings the Kaveri was not only the source of life-giving water but also of divine power. Along the river are three islands, formed where the water divides: from east to west, they are

Srirangam, Sivasamudram and Srirangapattana. These are the places where Vishnu sleeps upon the great serpent Sesha, when he is known as Sri Ranganatha, and on the islands are temples dedicated to the deity. The most magnificent is at Srirangam but all were recipients of past royal patronage; in 1610, Raja Wodeyar transferred his capital to Srirangapattana from Mysore after seizing the island from the Vijayanagara viceroy, Tirumala.

Given that the island of Srirangapattana was such a significant repository of divine power, Tipu would have been foolhardy to transfer his capital elsewhere. He continued the Wodeyars' patronage of the Sri Ranganatha temple, alongside which stood his main palace, and erected a Friday mosque. Haidar's tomb stood at the other end of the island, near the *sangam*, next to which Tipu built another, smaller mosque. Put simply, lordly benefaction, one of the defining characteristics of Indian kingship, was pragmatic in purpose. Along with their magnificent displays of power and wealth, kings were expected to be conspicuously pious. They made land grants, donated precious artefacts and mediated in religious disputes. In return, they could expect support for the legitimacy of their rule and prayers for the security and prosperity of the realm. Tipu behaved no differently: his generosity to temples, Sufi dargahs and mosques, as well as the great Math at Sringeri, are well documented, primarily through inscriptions and institutional records.

An idea of the number of Tipu's religious endowments across his realm can be gained by looking at *in'am* registers held in the Kozhikode Archives in Kerala. The records show that Tipu authorised sixty-seven grants of rent-free land, primarily to temples and mosques, solely for the taluks of Calicut, Ernad, Bettathnad and Chowghat. If we extrapolate that figure across the entire realm, it is clear that his patronage of such institutions was extensive. We know of several temples that hold objects donated by Tipu – the Sri Ranganatha temple at the capital received silver vessels, the Nanjundeshwara temple at Nanjangud has a jadeite linga said to have been installed on Tipu's orders, and inscriptions record that he gave elephants and silver vessels to the Narayanaswami temple in Melukote.

The Sringeri Math, with which Tipu maintained a close relationship, received gifts of valuable cloths and shawls, a silver palanquin and a pair of silver fly whisks. The importance of the Math to south Indian and Deccani rulers – both Hindu and Muslim – since its foundation in the eighth century, is demonstrated by the fact that it holds more than 200 copperplate grants and *sanads*, the earliest dating from the Ganga dynasty (c. 250–1000 CE). Tipu referred to the Math's Swami as the Jagadguru and, after the Marathas had raided the Math in 1792, he wrote in a letter that the culprits would 'suffer the consequences of their misdeeds at no distant date in the Kali age', concluding that 'treachery to gurus will undoubtedly result in the destruction of the line of descent'.

The political nature of religious patronage

was also the rationale behind acts of destruction. All across India, whenever a king conquered another, he signalled his victory by either seizing or destroying the religious sites with close ties to his victim – and it made no difference if conqueror and conquered were co-religionists. Just as Shaivite and Vaishnava dynasties in south India patronised mosques, dargahs and churches, they did not hesitate to capture the temples of their enemies and seize or destroy the images. The Cholas seized temple images from the Calukyas; and Vijayanagara's Krishnadevaraya, to celebrate his defeat of the Gajapati king, removed an image of Balakrishna from Udayagiri to the capital. We can see this process in operation with Tipu's demolition of the Varahaswami temple at Srirangapattana; after his death, the Wodeyars, in a statement of their own 'victory', relocated the ruined temple's image to Mysore town, which once again was serving as their capital. If Tipu's actions had been driven by religious rather than political motivation, he would not have allowed the Sri Ranganatha temple to continue to flourish within sight of his palace. It was the Wodeyars' direct association with Vishnu's boar incarnation that led to Tipu's demolition of the Varaha temple. Nor were Christians exempt from such treatment – the Venkataramana temple in Nagar (formerly Haidarnagar/Bednur) possesses a bell cast in Amsterdam in 1713. The presence of this oddity in a Hindu place of worship is due to Tipu's removal of it from a church in Malabar.

Similarly, Tipu did not discriminate against particular religious groups on the basis of their faith – indeed, his diwan or chief minister, Purnaiya, was a Hindu. As we have already seen, Tipu suspected the Kanara Christians of treachery and being in league with the British; the Nairs and the Kodavas, too, were punished for intriguing against him. And if there should be any doubt about what lay behind the treatment of such groups, the expulsion of the Mahdevis from Mysore in 1794 confirms the political character of such acts. This tight-knit Muslim community of several thousand mainly served in Tipu's army as horse soldiers, under the command of their own officers. That Tipu was in no way prejudiced against this sect is demonstrated by the fact that one of his four *vakils* to Istanbul, Ja'far Khan, was a Mahdevi; even so, he too was expelled in 1794. The stated reason for the community's expulsion was their refusal to obey Tipu's command to keep certain celebrations low-key – they were prone to noisy bouts of praying – as the festivities that year coincided with the return of the hostage princes from Madras. The more likely reason, however, was that Tipu suspected the Mahdevis of treason, with their festival disobedience merely the trigger for the order that they leave the kingdom. Interestingly, during the Fourth Anglo-Mysore War, many of them served under Arthur Wellesley as irregular horse, although it is not clear if this was a consequence of Tipu's treatment of them, or if Tipu had been correct in his original assumption of their disloyalty.

~

It is all too easy today, when we see outbreaks of violence based on religious difference, to interpret events from two hundred years ago in the same way. But the world we live in is the child of colonialism, which in the late eighteenth century was only beginning to make its mark on the subcontinent. It is also a post-industrial world, bearing the scars of social and economic disruption on a scale that could not have been imagined in pre-Raj India. Over the nineteenth century, the British imposed their will upon their colonial subjects, whether they liked it or not. When it suited them, they divided communities; Muslims, in particular, they regarded with suspicion due to their identification with the Mughals and the old antipathy between Christendom and Islam. Despite their claimed policy of staying out of religious affairs, the British emphasis on religious affiliation as a marker of identity meant that, under the Raj, the borders between different faith communities became more rigidly defined than they had been earlier.

Wherever human beings live side-by-side,

outbreaks of disagreement and sometimes even conflict are inevitable. The triggers for such clashes can only be found in the particular circumstance of each event – economic or social inequality, for example, practices that might offend a neighbouring group, political machinations, even personal disputes, all need to be considered as potential causes. We know of at least one occasion when Tipu himself was prepared to encourage a dispute between Muslims and Hindus in Pune, the Peshwa's territory, so as to weaken the Marathas at a time when relations between the two powers were less than friendly. In a letter to his *vakils* at the Peshwa's court, he wrote:

> Let the fire of discord, therefore, be kindled amongst them, to the end that they may, in this manner, waste [their strength upon] each other.

But within Mysore, as king, he would have been duty-bound to mediate such a dispute; it was not in his interest to exacerbate or fuel any kind of discord between his subjects. Nor was it in Tipu's interests to persecute them merely on the grounds of their religious affiliation; to do so would have been an act of frivolous self-indulgence. A peaceful realm was a productive realm, which in turn provided reliable revenue through taxation.

Whatever his enemies might have thought of him and despite how they portrayed him, Tipu took his responsibilities as king very seriously. In conformity with Islamic belief that the king is the embodiment of justice, Tipu presented himself as the *sultan-i 'adil*. All his actions and decisions were directed at fulfilling his duty as Haidar's heir – to secure the kingdom for posterity – and to rule according to the precepts of his faith and the expectations of his subjects. His princely education had equipped him for the challenge and he rose to meet it with alacrity. His intelligence and energy allowed him to build on Haidar's foundations and provide a credible alternative to, and barrier against, British incursions. Through the use of culturally familiar symbols of kingship and adherence to the norms of royal conduct, Tipu created an instantly recognisable identity as a legitimate and powerful king, one that even the British victors acknowledged when they transported his body through the streets of Srirangapattana to bury him as a prince.

6

The Man

Following Tipu's death, one of his munshis wrote for the British a short account of the late ruler's court. In it, he provided a brief description of Tipu's appearance:

> He was middle sized, of a tawny complexion, smooth open eyebrows, a broad ample forehead, dark grey eyes, a high nose, long neck, broad chest, slender waist, spindle legs, short mustachios, with his lower beard shaven.

Other commentators referred to his tendency to plumpness. A well-known contemporary portrait of Tipu (on the cover of this book), by an Indian artist and now in the collection of London's Victoria and Albert Museum, conforms to such a description. Seated in profile on a red *masnad*, Tipu is very much a king. He wears a green turban with a ruby and pearl *sarpech*, a green gown, three strands of pearls with ruby and pearl pendants, and a *kamarband* decorated with *babri* stripes. Across his shoulder is slung a belt from which hangs a fine sword in a red scabbard. The painting is thus an image of royalty, its purpose to portray its subject as a person of distinction – it does not, though, reveal his character. For that, we must search for clues within the documentary sources.

A study of the life of Tipu Sultan would be incomplete without a consideration of him as a man. So far, our focus has been on his identity as Haidar's son and as a king – the public face of Tipu, if you like. To find the human being behind the public mask requires a close reading of sources, especially between the lines, and an analysis of his language and behaviour in certain contexts. And we must be cautious in how we go about interpreting the documents. The temptation is to read him as we would a modern person, alive today, rather than someone from the eighteenth century. It is never possible to understand fully another human being – to 'get inside their head' – and from a distance of over two hundred years, it is even more difficult. Above all, we must not confuse the public with the private persona; nor should we believe the rhetoric of Tipu's enemies.

We already know that the British victors painted a picture of Tipu as a religious bigot and a tyrant. But we also know that contemporary evidence does not support such a portrayal, having seen instead how Tipu's actions conformed to the cultural and kingly conventions of the time. In this light and bearing in mind the caveats referred to above, let us now assess the personal side of this powerful man. In doing so, we will consider his religiosity, his dealings with other people, his relations with his family and his attitude towards women. We will examine the nature of his intelligence and the quality of his temperament;

and, given the manner of his death, there is a final question we might wish to ask: was Tipu courageous or was he merely stubborn?

~

Personal faith is not something that one can measure with any accuracy. The only test for genuine piety is to judge a person by their actions – how far they live according to the precepts of their religious creed, especially in their relations with other people. It is not enough that someone proclaim themselves devout if they do not demonstrate that fact apart from verbally. What then do Tipu's actions tell us?

The impression one gains from the historical record is that Tipu was a man who wished to live as a good Muslim, who put his faith into practice. His increased emphasis, following the 1792 defeat, upon the Islamic character of his rule implies a desire to appease God, that he feared he had incurred God's displeasure. This does not mean, though, that prior to the Third Anglo-Mysore War he had not tried to live piously. From the outset of his reign, it is clear that Tipu set about establishing himself as a just king. The introduction to what are known as his Commercial Regulations makes this clear:

> All praise and glory to the most high God, who, breathing life into a handful of clay, which was before inanimate, gave it the form of man; and who has raised some chosen individuals to rank and power, riches and rule, in order that they might administer to the feeble, the helpless, and the destitute, and promote the welfare of their people.
>
> In pursuance of this duty, we decree…

Here we have a precise articulation of Tipu's understanding of his duty as king, a product no doubt of his religious and philosophical education. Had he not been personally religious, it is unlikely he would have stated his purpose so succinctly. Furthermore, it does appear that in his dealings with his subjects, Tipu tried to be fair, to walk a middle path. His instructions to *amils*, *serishtadars* and *shamboges* are that they attend their department from nine in the morning until five at night, during which time they will compile and submit their accounts, after which 'they may then retire to rest.' When *ryots* fall behind in their dues, only those who can do so are required to pay in full, those who are poor can meet their debt by instalments, and any who have fled 'are to be encouraged to return, and the balances due are to be recovered by gentle means'.

Tipu also concerned himself with the moral character of his people. He tightened controls on the sale and consumption of liquor and prohibited the planting of bhang. He condemned prostitution (although did not ban it, probably recognising the futility of trying to do so) and frowned on excessive dancing. Both he and his father were affronted by the customs of the matrilineal Nairs: the minimal attire of the women shocked them, as did the practice of polyandry. That women took several husbands and appeared in public with their upper bodies uncovered would have challenged even the most moderate of Muslims. There is no evidence to suggest that either Haidar or Tipu considered offensive the naked form of the great statue of Gomateshwara Bahubali at Shravanabelgola – both rulers supported Jain institutions just as they did Hindu temples and Maths – so they cannot be regarded as iconoclasts or even prudes. But as Muslims, steeped in the concept of female modesty, the combination of multiple husbands and public toplessness was more than they could tolerate. Not surprisingly, they took steps to end both.

From these few examples, we can infer a desire on Tipu's part to follow the precepts of his faith, although not in an unreasonable manner. The case of the Nairs broke the limits of his forbearance, but in most matters he was pragmatic about what he could achieve. His morality was Islamic in foundation and he encouraged conversion where he could. Nowhere in the sources, however, does he come across as a fanatic. In fact, Tipu's attitude is primarily one of acceptance and understanding. This is most evident in his revenue and commercial regulations, which require his non-Muslim heads of departments to take oaths of service according to the conventions of their respective faiths. Additionally, the regulations instruct that when non-Muslim officials attend court they are to be fed appropriately; or, in other words, they should only be offered food permitted them.

Tipu's adherence to the terms of the treaties that he signed, and the expectation that others would do the same, suggest a man who kept his word. In March 1792, following the signing of the Treaty of Seringapatam, a British soldier involved in the war wrote in a letter that

> …some of our deep politicians say we place too much confidence in Tipoo, and that he will yet deceive us. I have observed nothing in his conduct lately, that should make us suspect him

> of unfair dealing, and I own myself to be among the many, who believe him sincere.

Tipu's treatment of his British prisoners of war also imply a man of integrity. Contrary to the apocryphal reports of extreme suffering, several captives' memoirs confirm that they were treated as well as they could have hoped in any similar situation in Europe. A soldier captured in early 1782 noted in his account Tipu's kindness and that the prisoners were given clothes and money. Tipu also

> gave strict orders to all his keeladars to be attentive to them during their march to Haidar's army, who was then lying at Conjeeveram.

Another soldier recounted that, on 4 June each year, the prisoners received a special meal, to celebrate the birthday of their king, George III.

In terms of his personal relationships, modern writers on Tipu generally agree that he was an affectionate family man and the sources support this assessment. There is no consensus, though, on the number of his offspring, or even of his wives. It is accepted that he married his first two wives – the daughter of Imam Sahib Bakhshi and Ruqayya Banu – on the same night in 1774, and that he took another wife in 1796, Khadija Zaman Begum, who died in childbirth in 1797. The British officer put in charge of the zenana following Tipu's death referred to a fourth wife, Buranti Begum, originally from Delhi, but no other contemporary sources mention her. The same officer reported the number of Tipu's surviving sons as twelve, the eldest being Fath Haidar, and his daughters as eight. The respective mothers of these children are not known. The zenana at Srirangapattana in 1799 held 601 women, 333 of whom were Tipu's and 268 his late father's, all guarded by eunuchs; this total included serving women as well as concubines and female family members. Among the last group was the wife of Abdul Karim, Tipu's brother, whom Haidar had married to the daughter of the Savanur Nawab in 1779. Abdul Karim is invariably described as 'feeble-minded' or 'half-witted', implying some kind of intellectual disability, and he had treated his wife cruelly; for her safety, Tipu had placed her with Haidar's remaining women.

Tipu's action in the case of his unhappy sister-in-law is of great interest, as it tells us something of his attitude towards women in general. Some men might have regarded the physical abuse of a wife as the husband's right; it seems this was not Tipu's view. Europeans were pruriently fascinated by Oriental harems, often allowing their imaginations to get the better of them, referring to the female inhabitants of such institutions as 'prisoners' and considering their lives to be unfortunate. Since these commentators rarely got anywhere near such institutions and almost never inside them (male physicians did sometimes enter, to minister to women who were concealed behind curtains), and the quality of the lives of royal women and their dependents was governed by the character of the ruler, their generalisations had no basis in reality. From what we can tell from the sources, Tipu liked women and even though his wives and concubines were entirely at his mercy – the latter sometimes purchased as slaves, sometimes the women of defeated enemies, sometimes entering the palace through a practice similar to what is known in Europe as *droit du seigneur*, the lord's right to take any of his subjects' daughters – there is no reason to believe that he mistreated them.

A clue to Tipu's attitude is found in one of his recorded dreams, dating from 1786. He wrote:

> It seemed to me as if a handsome young man, a stranger, came and sat down near me. I passed certain remarks in the manner in which one might, in a playful mood, talk to a woman.

Realising that he did not usually speak to people 'in such a playful manner', he was therefore not surprised when the youth loosed his hair from his turban and opened his robe to reveal breasts.

> I saw it was a woman. I immediately called and seated her and said to her: 'Whereas formerly I had only guessed you were a woman, and I had cut jokes with you, it is now definite that you are a woman in the dress of a man. My conjecture has come true.'

In his relations with women, then, it seems that Tipu's approach was light-hearted and flirtatious rather than forceful.

Tipu was also a conscientious father to his sons and his affection was apparently reciprocated. After the fall of Srirangapattana, prize agents were put in charge of the distribution of the booty, one of whom later wrote a memoir. In it he describes how one of the princes had been allowed to look in on the agents as they sorted through Tipu's substantial library. 'Only see,' the distressed young man remarked, 'how these hogs are allowed to contaminate my father's books.' For Muslims, a special quality attaches to the written word and the discovery of non-believers handling the many treasured volumes could only have magnified the trauma of Tipu's death.

Tipu took a close interest in his sons' education, even considering in the 1780s sending one of them to France for that purpose. His *vakils* raised the idea with the French government when in Paris but the onset of the Third Anglo-Mysore War in 1790 apparently put an end to the plan. As his own father had done, Tipu was raising his sons as princes. He personally oversaw their reading, sourcing works from his library for their tuition. During their stay in Madras, when the princes Abdul Khaliq and Muizuddin were taken as hostages, Ghulam Ali Khan and Ali Reza Khan were expected to monitor their conduct. In a letter to Ghulam Ali, Tipu informed him that he should 'take care in instructing my sons to speak slow [*sic*] and properly to Lord Cornwallis'.

A British officer, who was present, has left an account of the first meeting between Cornwallis and the boys that confirms their good manners and refinement:

> The Princes were dressed in long white muslin gowns, and red turbans. They had several rows of large pearls round their necks, from which was suspended an ornament consisting of a ruby and an emerald of considerable size, surrounded by large brilliants; and in their turbans, each had a sprig of rich pearls. Bred up from their infancy with infinite care, and instructed in their manners to imitate the reserve and politeness of age, it astonished all present to see the correctness and propriety of their conduct.

The following day, Abdul Khaliq and Muizuddin, accompanied by the *vakils*, had another meeting with Cornwallis:

> The youngest [aged five]...appeared to be the favourite with the vakeels; and at the desire of Gullam Ally, repeated or rather recited some verses in Arabic, which he had learned by heart from the Koran, and afterwards some verses in Persian, which he did with great ease and confidence, and shewed he had made great progress in his education.

Tipu's pride at his little son's poise and ability can only be imagined.

The boys' two-year absence must have been a worrying period for Tipu, despite the governor-general's reassurance that he would be as a father to them. On the day of the princes' departure from Srirangapattana – delayed, as we have seen, by the family's distress – Tipu had stood on the fort's ramparts to watch them go. It surely felt as if a very part of him had been taken captive.

～

As Badshah, Tipu aspired to universal kingship and demonstrated the extent of his influence through the possession of all manner of exotica and rarities, a common practice amongst Indian rulers of the time. Works of European manufacture, such as clocks, watches and other automata, were especially prized, and the acquisition of foreign women, animals and plants was also part of the process. For some monarchs, it was enough merely to own curious items and beings but in Tipu's case it went beyond mere collection. It is evident that the Mysore ruler possessed an inquiring mind and he was clearly fascinated by such things as the microscope that he had coveted as a young man near Madras. His relationship with the French at Pondicherry gave him a ready source for objects that captured his attention. In 1786, the governor David Charpentier de Cossigny sent Tipu a barometer; later, Tipu wrote asking the Frenchman to arrange the translation into Persian of a book on the thermometer, which should then be forwarded to him.

Such intellectual curiosity implies an above-average intelligence and when one reads Tipu's letters and administrative documents the breadth of his knowledge is striking. For example, on learning that a deposit of lead has been found within the realm, he instructs an official to look for silver, as the two minerals often occur together, not something the ordinary 'man in the street' might be expected to know. He was also well informed about the history of northern India – Aurangzeb's reign, for instance; the specifics of the growing British influence in Bengal and Awadh – and he kept abreast of current affairs. Naturally, it was in his interest to do so; yet his understanding of complex issues and the minute attention he paid to all aspects of government betray a man of lively intellect and energy. And in his prediction that, unhindered, the British would become increasingly entrenched on the subcontinent, to the detriment of its inhabitants, there is a kind of wisdom.

But in the end, for all his intelligence and drive, Tipu was defeated. Was he perhaps not so wise after all? Should he have gone down the path that the Nizam had taken, signing a subsidiary alliance with the British? We should remember, though, that Tipu was not the last Indian power to resist the East India Company and its forces; a number of Maratha chiefs continued to fight, for instance, and the Sikhs hung on into the 1840s – so in that sense, he was not unique. However, with the benefit of hindsight, and given the extensive mythologising that began as soon as he died, it is all too easy to regard Tipu's death as inevitable, to see stubborn intransigence as the cause of his demise. But by 1798, with the failure of his mission to Mauritius and the publication in Calcutta of Governor Malartic's proclamation, the Mysore ruler realised that he was bereft of allies and sought negotiations with the British governor-general. It was too late. Lord Mornington was in a belligerent frame of mind and saw his opportunity to subdue Tipu once and for all. Neither man, however, anticipated that the conflict would end with Tipu's death.

Lord Mornington's correspondence with his officers makes it clear that he was expecting to force Mysore's surrender, followed by an agreement along the lines of that made with Hyderabad, and, had Tipu not been cut down unexpectedly following the breaching of the fort, it is likely that he would have agreed to negotiate. He had not had a chance to evacuate his family, although the British found signs that he had planned to do so, and he would have done all he could to keep them safe – to lose one's women to the enemy was the ultimate ignominy for an Indian ruler. As humiliating as it would have been for Tipu to sign a subsidiary treaty with the British, nothing that we know about him indicates that he would have sacrificed his family and his life for no purpose.

Tipu was undoubtedly a courageous man – his exploits in battle prove that beyond question – but the best way to describe him is as a preserver: throughout his reign, his goal had been to retain the territories Haidar had acquired, not to expand them. Writing to potential allies in the mid 1790s, Tipu had made it clear that his aims were twofold: to expel the British from India and to regain the districts he had ceded in 1792. It is pure romanticism to think that Tipu would have preferred to go down fighting rather than surrender – if that had been the case, he would have done so at the end of the Third-Anglo Mysore War; instead, he chose to sign a treaty with his foe. He was not the victim of a stubborn nature. Rather, as we have seen, he was a pragmatist – he had asked to negotiate but the governor-general had refused. Misfortune or fate, his death was the result of a confluence of events: Lord Mornington's wish to attack Mysore in place of diplomacy; Tipu's decision to leave his palace on being told of the death of a senior officer; his instinctive response to lash out at the soldier trying to rob him. Contrary to some British claims, he was mourned by many of his subjects, a large number of whom lined the streets to bid farewell to him. A thunderstorm crashed over them as his body was interred in the Gumbaz, the tomb Tipu had built for Haidar and where he and his father lie together to this day.

Appendices

APPENDIX A

An *ikram-nama*, or written testament of allegiance, indicating the kinds of penalties transgressors might face in Tipu's Mysore, found amongst documents at Srirangapattana in 1799. Translator: Colonel William Kirkpatrick.

I will not do [any] one thing without the pleasure of your blessed majesty; Lord of Benefits; (or my bountiful Lord). If I do, let me be punished in whatever manner may seem fitting to your auspicious mind. – One article

If in the affairs of the Sircar, I should commit theft, or be guilty of forgery great or small let me, as the due punishment thereof be strangled. – One article

If I be guilty of prevarication [illegible], or misrepresentation or of treachery, deceit or fraud the proper punishment thereof is the same strangulation. – One article

Without the orders of the Presence, I will not receive from anyone nuzzers &c. nor will I take things from any person [meaning perhaps forcibly]. If I do, let my nose be cut off, and let me be driven out of the City. – One article

With whomsoever, excepting on the affairs of the Sircar, I shall hold any other discourse, or be guilty of treachery &c. let me in punishment thereof be stretched on a cross. – One article

Whenever a Country shall be committed to my charge by the Sircar, and an army be placed under my command (or be stationed with me) I will carry on all business regarding the same, with the advice and through the medium of such confidential person as may be appointed [for the purpose] by the Sircar: and if I transact such affairs through any other channel but his, let me be strangled. – One article

If there be any writing business for correspondence or any occasion to buy, or give anything: or any letters should arrive from any place, I will do nothing [in such matters] without the concurrence and advice of the person appointed by the Sircar. – One article

I have written and given these few article of my own free will: keeping the contents whereof in my heart's remembrance, I will act in each article accordingly. If I forget this, and act in another [a different] manner let me be punished agreeably to the foregoing writing.

Source: *Kirkpatrick Papers*, British Library, MSS Eur.F.228/41.

APPENDIX B

Extract from Tipu's military manual, *Fath ul-Mujahidin*, composed at the start of his reign – very likely under his guidance – by one of his courtiers, Zein ul-Abidin Shastari, and distributed to all officers and senior officials.

Requisite Information for Dispositions of War.

It is requisite before the Commencement of a Battle, and kindling up the Conflagration of a hot Engagement, that the General should himself advance in Front, to view the Field of Action, and reconnoitre the Ground of the Enemy's

Encampment, to know whether his Adversary has taken Refuge in a strong Situation; such as Shelter from the Thicket of Trees, the Bottom of a Hill, or having running Water near them; in such a Dilemma, it is improper to give Battle; but if there should be urgent Causes for it, you must then lay your Troops in Ambush to discover whether your Enemies [*sic*] Security is in Front, on One or both Flanks; it is then necessary to detach the Cavalry, to amuse the Enemy with slight Skirmishes, in order to draw them from their Retreat, and near your own Army; which when you have done, first open your Guns and small Arms, so as to reach them; then cautiously prepare yourself for a smart Engagement with your Cannon and small Arms. But if an auxiliary Army should be drawn up in an open Plain to assist them, you must then form your Troops into Three contiguous Divisions, and after a Volley of Cannon and small Arms, charge with Bayonets upon the Enemy; but if the aiding Body should be so powerful, it is then improper to bring on a general Engagement; but to commence an easy Retreat, which must be effected in this Manner: by Choosing some of the smartest of your Guns, and with them begin a Cannonade; also station your Cavalry of Observation, at a respective Distance from yourself, and some remote Place from the Enemy, in order to give you instantaneous Intelligence of the Enemy's Halting and Motion. Whenever your Adversary prepares to charge the Cavalry, order then the Guns to be drawn off; and if the Enemy makes a Halt, do you likewise halt: Give Orders to the Artillery to be in Readiness, that wherever the Enemy may encamp, it is preferable to surprize them in the Night; if the Adversary should be near you, about Three o'Clock in the Morning, is the Time; but if at some Distance, a little after Dusk, softly run out the lightest of your Guns, and move off gently with all Silence, in order that the Beating of the Infantry's Feet, and the Clattering of the Horses' Hoofs, in the March, may not be heard; and also that the Detachment may not have Intercourse, or Conversation with one another, until they have reached the Enemy; which having come within Bow or Musket-shot, to give a general Discharge of Cannon and small Arms, and immediately to charge their Encampment; but permit none of your Detachment to go in Search of Plunder and Booty; because, when fighting Men throw aside their Arms for Avarice of Riches and Rapine, it has often been proved by Experience, that the Enemy have rallied their Troops, and returned again to the Charge, which in such precarious Times, have been attended with embarrassing Consequences.

Source: *The Military Maxims and Observations of Tippoo Sultan; containing General Rules for a Commander*, W. Clarke: London, 1791, pp. 19–21.

APPENDIX C

Extracts from Draft Statement of Instructions (*Hukmnama*) [to the *vakils* Ghulam Ali Khan, Nurullah Khan, Lutf Ali Khan and Ja'far Khan] for Negotiations with the Ruler (*Khundkar*) of Turkey (*Rum*) [i.e. the Ottoman Sultan Abdul Hamid I].

You should … proceed to Islambol (Istanbul), and present to the Ruler of Turkey one elephant with silver canopy, one roofed palanquin, one finger-ornament (*sarpanj*), one astrolabe (*falaki*), a bejewelled medallion, twenty-one embroidered robes, etc., and also give robes to the Ruler's ministers in accordance with the separate memorandum (*yad-dasht*).

You should say that the country of Bengal, which has revenues of twenty crore of rupees, the country of Carnatic with revenues of three crore of rupees, and the country of Surat, Gujarat, etc., with three crore of rupees, in total rupees twenty-six crore, which belonged to the emperor of Hindustan, has been seized by the English, by use of collusion with and [inciting] treachery of the governors of these territories. Twenty-five to thirty years have passed since then. They have invited many Muslims to join infidelity and have converted them to their own religion. ... When the dominance of infidelity reached its acme, the ardour for Islam was inflamed, and our master [Haidar Ali] launched an attack on the faithless Christians, sent thousands of them to the lowest hell, and made many of them captives and prisoners. After two years he gave crores [of rupees] in help and lakhs [of men] in reinforcement to the French, who had been expelled from the country of Hindustan at the hands of the English, and summoned them from the port of Mauritius, which is an island of the ocean, and gave them their old places ... Finally, he conducted a great war for four years, and for the sake of the strength of the Muhammadan (*Ahmadi*) faith, thousands of high commanders and lakhs of soldiers tasted martyrdom in the four years of war with the infidels [the English]. The faithless Christians became helpless and sent their high representatives to our master and sought peace with expressions of helplessness and importunity; and the French mediated on their behalf. There was no option but to accept peace. Other factors also came about to make the conclusion of peace expedient. The Marathas, owing to their sympathy for infidelity, had become allies of the English. Owing to this, concluding peace with the English, [our present master, Tipu] is engaged in destroying and suppressing the Marathas, and by God's aid they shall receive a satisfactory chastisement. By His grace, this Government has large forces on land. For the destruction and suppression of the Christians, ships are needed.

By God's grace this Government has large resources for building ships and there are many safe havens for ships under this Government. but owing to the six months of the rainy season, the ships cannot remain at sea owing to storms. Therefore, our master wishes that if he [the ruler of Turkey] gives the port of Basra on farm (*ijara*), the fixed amount would be paid to the [Ottoman] Ruler's government and [our master] would keep his ships in the safe haven. [This did not occur, either because the Sultan did not agree to the request, or because the request was never made. KB] …

In return for it [Basra], any of the ports of this Government that is chosen [by the Ottoman Ruler] will be given over to the servants of the [Ottoman] ruler. Merchants, etc., will then travel to and fro taking the fine commodities and goods of this country to the country of Turkey (*Rum*), and bringing the rarities of the country of Turkey to this country. …

By the grace of God, innumerable muskets and cannon-pieces are manufactured in the country of the Government. Thus persons accompanying us carry those very muskets: [The Ottoman Ruler] should give us better craftsmen to manufacture muskets, cannon-pieces, clocks (*gharial*), glass, chinaware and mirrors to accompany us [to our country]. This would be a source of pleasure to our master and also of the strengthening of the community's faith (*din-i milli*). The Christians who have obtained dominance in [our] country, have become dominant over and occupied [our] country owing to these very things. You, who are a great King of Muslims, should strive by all means to strengthen the True Religion. Whatever is required from the Government of our master will be furnished. By His grace, our master is in possession of all things needed. But the faithless Christians need to receive chastisement from the King of Muslims [the ruler of Turkey]. …

Written on … Thursday, 14th Muharram, 12[00] Hijri [17 November 1785], camp Zafarabad.

Source: 'The Diplomatic Vision of Tipu Sultan: Briefs for Embassies to Turkey and France, 1785-86', Iqbal Husain, trans., in Irfan Habib, ed., *State and Diplomacy under Tipu Sultan: Documents and Essays*, Tulika: New Delhi, 2001, pp. 40–42.

APPENDIX D

Extracts from Draft Statement of Instructions (*Hukmnama*) [to the *vakils* Ghulam Ali Khan, Nurullah Khan, Lutf Ali Khan and Ja'far Khan] for Negotiations with the King of France [In the end, Tipu decided to send a separate embassy to France. KB]

[The ambassadors are to make the following representations to the King of France:]

During the last thirty years, the English have taken possession of land worth rupees twenty-six crores [in annual revenue] in the country of Carnatic, Bengal, Surat and Gujarat including

Machhili Bandar (Masulipatam), etc., through collusion with the officials of the King of Hindustan, by means of deceit and treachery, and have committed much oppression and tyranny on Muslims and others. ... They have seized Pondicherry two or three times, and made most of the French there their captives and prisoners, and inflicted extreme tyranny and oppression on the French people. All this must have been brought to your knowledge through letters and oral reports by your servants. Our mentioning the matter again is superfluous. In fact, the English over six or seven years ago marched against Pondicherry and, having forcibly brought it under their control, destroyed it. They sent ships to seize the port of Mahe, which is within the territory of this Government. At that time our master [Haidar Ali] was engaged in an expedition into another country. He therefore wrote to the English. ... Despite repeated writing from our master, the English did not withdraw and occupied the said port. The moment he heard of this, our master was enraged. He withdrew from a country worth rupees five crores which he had brought under his possession from another ruler, – both from it and from the enemy's fort that he had laid siege to and which was close to being captured. Without returning to the capital, but by-passing it, he marched into the country of the Carnatic. ... The army of our Government captured or killed nearly three-fourths [lit. three parts] of the army of the enemy's forces. ...

In the end, in accordance with the will of God, he [Haidar Ali] died in the vicinity of Arcot. At that time His Highness, our master's son, let God make his authority eternal, was engaged in chastising the English in the territory of Calicut. After chastising them, the moment he heard this news, he proceeded by forced marches and entered the victorious camp [of Haidar Ali's army]. ...

...During the four years of the war the English had repeatedly requested our Government that it should not help the French: 'We [the English] will ourselves conclude peace [with you] and will be obedient to you and will withdraw from Trichinopoly and other territories of the Government as well as the country of Carnatic.' We (Tipu's Government) did not accept this, in consideration of the feelings of the King France, and so had to bear the burden of expenditure of crores [of rupees]. Now the French, without informing our Government had concluded peace and set right their own affairs while spoiling ours. Now, except for war, no peace was acceptable. A letter of this substance was sent to Monsieur Bussy [Marquis de Bussy, commander of French forces in India. K.B]. Monsieur Bussy sent Mr Sadleir [Anthony Sadlier K.B.], the second Governor of Chenna-pattan [Madras K.B.], with his own letters by the land route, to solicit peace. Mr Sadleir made a journey of two months to reach our master at the port of Koryal [Mangalore K.B.]. He expressed much helplessness and importunity. ... At last, in view of Monsieur Bussy's pleadings, the expressions of helplessness and importunity by Mr Sadleir, and the exigencies of time, he (Tipu) agreed to conclude peace.

Now we have travelled such a long distance, which none of the men of our country from the beginning of time till date has traversed, in order to come to this land. [We have done so] only to disclose the breach of promise and acts of disloyalty committed by your servants, since these unreasonable acts have perhaps been committed without your knowledge. Otherwise, this is not [according to] the ways of statesmen and persons of nobility. We hope to take a written statement of pledge and promise from you personally, and obtain knowledge of your inclinations, so that we may gird our loins to punish and destroy your enemies, who have always been [hostile] to you, since olden days. …

Written on … 14th Muharram, Thursday, 12[00] Hijri [17 November 1785].

Source: 'The Diplomatic Vision of Tipu Sultan: Briefs for Embassies to Turkey and France, 1785-86', Iqbal Husain, trans., in Irfan Habib, ed., *State and Diplomacy under Tipu Sultan: Documents and Essays*, Tulika: New Delhi, 2001, pp. 42–49.

Quotation Sources

P. 8. 'fix [its] talons': cited in Kate Brittlebank, *Tipu Sultan's Search for Legitimacy: Islam and Kingship in a Hindu Domain*, Oxford University Press: Delhi, 1997, p. 27.

'never doubted ...': cited in Brittlebank, *Tipu Sultan's Search for Legitimacy*, p. 21.

P. 32. 'Hyder, who passionately...': Maistre de la Tour, cited in Brittlebank, *Tipu Sultan's Search for Legitimacy*, p. 23.

P. 57. 'pepper, sandalwood...': cited in M.P. Sridharan, 'Tipu's Letters to French Officials, in *India History Congress*

Proceedings, 45, 1984, p. 506.

P. 66. 'a prince of ...': cited in Mohibbul Hasan, *History of Tipu Sultan*, 2nd ed., The World Press: Calcutta, 1971, p. 148.

P. 78. 'The Maratha army...': Mahmud Husain, trans., *The Dreams of Tipu Sultan*, Pakistan Historical Society: Karachi, n.d., p. 35. Edited for accuracy.

P. 79. 'I went to the Maulana...'; 'That very night...': Husain, *The Dreams of Tipu Sultan*, pp. 96–97.

P. 99. 'suffer the consequences'; 'treachery to gurus': cited in Brittlebank, *Tipu Sultan's Search for Legitimacy*, p. 130.

P. 104. 'Let the fire...': cited in Brittlebank, *Tipu Sultan's Search for Legitimacy*, p. 35.

P. 109. 'He was middle sized...': Munshi M. Qasim, An Account of Tipu Sultan's Court, British Library, MSS Eur.C.10.

P. 113. 'All praise and ...': cited in Nikhiles Guha, *Pre-British State System in South India: Mysore 1761-1799*, Popular Prakashan: Calcutta, 1985, p. 171.

P. 114. 'they may then...': Burrish Crisp, trans., *The Mysorean Revenue Regulations*, Calcutta, 1792, p. 24.

'are to be encouraged ...': Crisp, *Mysorean Revenue Regulations*, p. 28.

P. 116. 'some of our ...': Francis Skelly to Charles Stuart, 25 March 1792 in Francis Skelly, *Letters & Miscellaneous Papers etc, c. 1785-92*, British Library, MSS Eur.D.877.

P. 117. 'gave strict orders...': cited in Hasan, *History of Tipu Sultan*, p. 18.

Pp. 120–21. 'It seemed to me ...'; 'in such a ...'; 'I saw it was ...': Husain, *The Dreams of Tipu Sultan*, pp. 63-4.

P. 121. 'Only see ...': David Price, *Memoirs of the Early Life and Service of a Field Officer on the Retired List of the Indian Army*, London, 1839, p. 446.

P. 122. 'take care in ...': cited in Denys Forrest, *Tiger of Mysore: The Life and Death of Tipu Sultan*, Chatto & Windus: London, 1970, p. 212.

Pp. 123–24. 'The Princes were...'; 'The youngest...': Alexander Dirom, *A Narrative of the Campaign in India which terminated the War with Tippoo Sultan in 1792*, London, 1793, pp. 229, 231.

References

Kate Brittlebank, *Tipu Sultan's Search for Legitimacy: Islam and Kingship in a Hindu Domain*, Oxford University Press: Delhi, 1997

Anne Buddle, *Tigers Round the Throne: The Court of Tipu Sultan (1750-1799)*, Zamana Gallery: London, 1990

Richard H. Davis, *Lives of Indian Images*, Princeton University Press: Princeton, N.J., 1997

Mohibbul Hasan, *History of Tipu Sultan*, 2nd ed., The World Press: Calcutta, 1971

George Michell, ed., *Eternal Kaveri*, Marg Publications: Mumbai, 1999

Susan Stronge, *Tipu's Tigers*, V & A Publishing: London, 2009

Major Regional Powers in the Deccan and South India in the Eighteenth Century

Prepared by the Juggernaut Books editorial team

Mysore (1565–1947): The Wodeyars had ruled Mysore as petty chiefs under the suzerainty of the Vijayanagar Empire since the end of the fourteenth century. They established independent rule when Vijayanagar collapsed in 1565. The seventeenth century was a period of expansion for the kingdom of Mysore as it annexed territories in present-day south Karnataka and Tamil Nadu. In 1761, the Wodeyar king Krishna Raja II admitted defeat after Haider Ali took Srirangapattana. The Wodeyars' rule over Mysore, though by then a much-diminished state that had entered into a subsidiary alliance with the British, was re-established after Tipu Sultan was killed.

Bednur (1499–1763): The nayakas of Bednur, also known as the nayakas of Keladi and the kings of Ikkeri, were vassals of Vijayanagar, and became independent rulers after the fall of that empire in 1565. Their kingdom was based out of Keladi in Shimoga, Karnataka, and covered at its peak significant parts of the Malnad area of the Western Ghats in present-day Karnataka, coastal Karnataka, parts of north Kerala, and some plains of the Tungabhadra river. It was annexed by Haidar Ali and became part of Mysore in 1763.

Carnatic (1692–1853): The Carnatic region of south India was ruled by the nawab of the Carnatic, also known as the nawab of Arcot after its capital city in present-day Tamil Nadu, under the

Mughal subahdar of the Deccan. The nawabship was established by Aurangzeb as a reward for his nobleman and military general for wresting Gingee fort from the Marathas. Due to the vacuum left by the fall of Vijayanagar in 1565, the nawab of the Carnatic gained control of a vast territory south of the Krishna. The nawabs had to contend with challenges from the Marathas as well as the interference of the British and French, especially in matters of succession. Haidar Ali allied with the British during the siege of Tiruchirappalli in 1751–52 during one such succession dispute but later switched sides to the French due to British broken promises. When the thirteenth nawab died without children, the British applied the Doctrine of Lapse and annexed the kingdom.

Hyderabad (1724–1948): After the death of Aurangzeb, the Mughal empire was enfeebled, its treasury seriously depleted, and it began to break up. The Mughal viceroy in the Deccan, Asaf Jah, declared himself the nizam ul-mulk of

Hyderabad in south-central Deccan and founded the Asaf Jahi dynasty that would rule Hyderabad till Independence. Hyderabad fought a series of battles with the Marathas and signed a subsidiary alliance with the British in 1798. In the Third Anglo-Mysore War (1790–92), in which Tipu lost almost half his territory and had two of his sons taken hostage, Hyderabad was allied with the victorious British.

Travancore (1729–1949): At its peak, the kingdom of Travancore covered most of present-day south and central Kerala as well as Kanyakumari in present-day Tamil Nadu. Travancore's history can be traced back to Marthanda Varma. During his reign (1729–1758), he expanded his kingdom from Kanyakumari in the south to Kochi in the north, defeating the Dutch East India Company and a union of Nair feudal lords to establish the kingdom of Travancore. Tipu's aggression in his border dispute with Travancore in 1790 led to the Third Anglo-Mysore War.

The Maratha Empire (1674–1818): Maratha power rose as a result of the exertions of Shaji Bhonsle and his son Shivaji, a one-time Mughal mansabdar, both of whom rebelled against their overlords: variously the sultans of Ahmadnagar and Bijapur, and the Mughal emperor.

The second Maratha peshwa or prime minister, a hereditary position, devised the system of semi-autonomous Maratha clans or the Maratha Confederacy around the 1720s. The Marathas put up fierce opposition to Mysore, first under the Wodeyars and then under Tipu's father Haidar Ali and Tipu himself. Haidar Ali in fact distinguished himself when he was serving in the Wodeyar army, in action against the Marathas in which he took the city of Devanhalli, where Tipu was born. Though the Marathas and Mysore under Haidar Ali were some-time allies – in the First Anglo-Mysore War – the relationship was one of bitter rivalry and contest. In the third Anglo-Mysore war (1790–1792) Tipu lost substantial territories to the Marathas. The Third Anglo-Maratha War resulted in the loss of Maratha independence in 1818.

The British: From 1600, when the English East India Company was granted a charter by Queen Elizabeth I till about the turn of the seventeenth century, the Company made significant inroads in India. By 1616, it had secured permission from the Mughal emperor to establish a factory at Surat. The British were subsequently able to set up a settlement in Madras in 1639 which came to be known as Fort St George in 1642; in Hughli in 1658; in Bombay in 1668; and at Fort William in Calcutta in 1690.

By 1757, the English East India Company had established armies at each of its three presidencies: Bombay, Madras and Calcutta. The eighteenth century saw a rapid increase in the strength of the British army in India: from 18,000 troops in 1763 to 102,000 in 1796. The British fought a series of four wars against Haidar and Tipu: in 1769, 1780–1784, 1790–1792 and 1799. In the last two wars the British defeated Tipu, who was killed in the 1799 battle.

The French: The French Compagnie des Indes Orientales established its main base in India in Pondicherry in 1674, south of the English East India Company's settlement at Fort St George. Subsequently, it set up additional factories in Surat and Chandernagore. The French governor general of India between 1742 and 1754 was Joseph Francois Dupleix, a bitter rival of the English East India Company's Robert Clive, who was governor of the presidency of Fort William between 1757–1760 and again from 1765–1766. A series of three Anglo-French Carnatic Wars were fought in the middle of the eighteenth century. Haidar Ali and Tipu by and large regarded the French as their allies, sharing with them a common enemy in the British.

AN EXTENSIVE LIBRARY

Including fresh, new, original Juggernaut books from the likes of Sunny Leone, Praveen Swami, Husain Haqqani, Umera Ahmed, Rujuta Diwekar and lots more. Plus, books from partner publishers and loads of free classics. Whichever genre you like, there's a book waiting for you.

CRUCIBLES OF SIN
HITESHA
Can a Geek ever find Love?
Finding Juliet
Toffee
Mary Shelley
Frankenstein
A FAROOQ RESHI INVESTIGATION
COLD FLAKE
PRAVEEN SWAMI
A Psychiatrist's Guide To Heartbreak
How to Heal Your Broken Heart
DR SHYAM BHAT
MOIN and THE MONSTER
stories of women from the ganglands
S. Hussain Zaidi with Jane Borges
Foreword by Vishal Bharadwaj
UMERA AHMED
Nowhere Girl
A Story of Love & Forgiveness
THE BEHEADING
ABHEEK BARUA
THE Peshwa
The Lion and the Stallion
THE INVISIBLE WOMAN
SAURBH KATYAL
ANGRY BIRDS FAN? READ THE BOOK!
ANGRY BIRDS TOONS
TOONS TALES
ARCHANA SABOO
ADIKOOL
in
#AfricanAdventures
Tarana Khan
DON'T FALL IN LOVE
Vandana Shankar
KHUSHWANT SINGH
WE INDIANS

DON'T JUST READ; INTERACT

We're changing the reading experience from passive to active.

Ask authors questions

Get all your answers from the horse's mouth. Juggernaut authors actually reply to every question they can.

Rate and review

Let everyone know of your favourite reads or critique the finer points of a book – you will be heard in a community of like-minded readers.

Gift books to friends

For a book-lover, there's no nicer gift than a book personally picked. You can even do it anonymously if you like.

Enjoy new book formats

Discover serials released in parts over time, picture books including comics, and story-bundles at discounted rates. And coming soon, audiobooks.

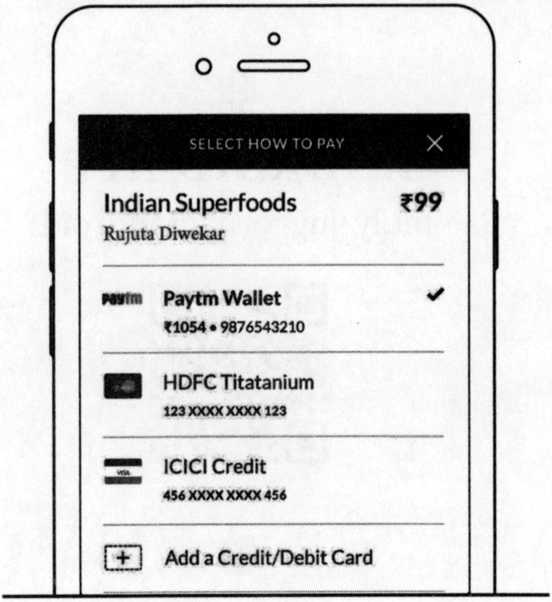

Paytm Wallet, Cards & Apple Payments

On Android, just add a Paytm Wallet once and buy any book with one tap. On iOS, pay with one tap with your iTunes-linked debit/credit card.

Click the QR Code with a QR scanner app or type the link into the Internet browser on your phone to download the app.

ANDROID APP

bit.ly/juggernautandroid

iOS APP

bit.ly/juggernautios